Let's Get The GAY THING Straight

by Gary Mortara

LET'S GET THE GAY THING STRAIGHT

For further information, write Gary Mortara,
577 Manor Blvd., San Leandro, CA. 94579

Editing and Interior design:
Gary Mortara
Cover design by Mike Pine

ISBN: 978-0-615-53237-0
Printed in Colombia

TABLE OF CONTENTS

Preface

Chapter 1
    Please Forgive Us

Chapter 2
    The Path Less Traveled

Chapter 3
    Is There Scientific Proof?

Chapter 4
    What Would Jesus Say?

Chapter 5
    The Modern Day Sex Revolution

Chapter 6
    What Does the Bible Really Teach About Homosexuality?

Chapter 7
    The Seduction of Masturbation

Chapter 8
    Coming Out

Notes
Biblical Quotations

PREFACE

The very fact that you are reading this page tells me that you are interested in the contents of this book. Let me give them to you, so that the purpose of reading this book in its entirety, will be accomplished. Before you start, though, please fight the tendency to disagree with the first thing you find to disagree with. Since the book is now in your possession, grant yourself the privilege of reading all the pages so you will be able to form a complete and thorough opinion.

I know you have one already, an opinion, that is. Otherwise, why would you even be reading this book? You want to see if this author lines up with your perspective. I understand. But I also believe that you are fair enough with yourself, that if you were to learn something new, you would allow it to further shape your opinion on this topic. Be that as it may, let me give you the contents of this book in short form here, then I will elaborate on them in each successive chapter.

And thanks for being open minded!

Topics to be discussed:

a) A deep and sincere apology from the Christian community for the way we have acted towards the gay community.

b) Possible paths that can lead to being gay.

c) Would the gay community welcome Jesus if he visited them and just wanted to hang out?

d) Scientific studies on the gay gene found in people.

e) What does the Bible say about homosexuality?

f) Did the sexual revolution really start in the 1960's?

g) Should there be rules governing our sexual practices, or should it be, "do as you see fit"

h) What are some of the reasons why people masturbate?

I) Let's say I wanted to go straight - can I, really?

These are the main points I will be discussing in this book. Of course, there are many other things in these pages which will be brought out in detail, but these are the topics people have shown the most interest in from my investigations. It is my desire in this book to give a more rounded view (looking at it from a few different perspectives) of this controversial issue about the gay life and Christianity.

My reason for writing this book

It wasn't until someone I knew shared with me the struggle he was having, knowing what God had said in his Word about homosexuality, and yet feeling he had no control over the fact that he was attracted to the same sex, that I began to seriously investigate and understand what many gay people are dealing with. As I spent many hours talking with this person and rethinking my own beliefs, I now hope to share with you what I have learned and discovered in the pages that follow. I believe we are all going to learn some very interesting things; I know I did.

I also want to make a clear distinction between God loving people, and Him being pleased with them. These are not one and the same. Yes, God loves everybody, much like parents love all their children. However, even the most loving parents can be disappointed in the decisions and behaviors of their children. When a child acts in ways the parent clearly does not approve of, parents can be saddened, let down, and even angered by the choices the child has made. Even a police officer who may really like someone, including a family member, will still put that person under arrest if he breaks the law.

That is how God feels when people make decisions and continue in behaviors which are clearly a violation of His known will and commands. This goes for the Pope and the prisoner. God has shown His love for people by sending His son to die for us all. Yet, He wants us to live pleasing and obedient lives, according to His Word and His will. This goes for the Christian and the non-Christian, for the straight person and the gay. Does He loves us all? Yes! Is He pleased with all of us? I will let you decide.

So with that, let's begin.

SPECIAL THANKS

A special thanks to my dear friend Hillary Flowers for all her tedious labor in editing this book. Your insights, corrections, ideas, and knowledge were exactly what was needed to accomplish this project. Thank you for believing in what God had put in my heart to do. You're the best !

I have to say thanks to my longtime friend and science teacher Chuck Vonderheid for the research he provided for me from the scientific community. Thanks, my brother.

Thanks to the congregation at Faith Fellowship for praying for me and pushing me to see this project through to the end. The conversations we had shaped the focus of this book.

Thanks to my son Jonathan, for all the deep conversations we have had and for challenging your old man with new thoughts. I love you, son.

A special Thank You to Eda Dozek for all your efforts on the final editing of this book. Couldn't have completed this without you.

CHAPTER
1

PLEASE FORGIVE US

Please forgive us.

We owe you the deepest and most sincere apology. We are wrong. We have sinned against you. We have not been fair. We have not represented Christ properly to you. We have judged you without knowing all the facts. We have had superior attitudes toward you that haven't represented the true heart of Christ. We have hurt you and turned you away from the gospel of Jesus Christ. I apologize for the we.

Who is "we".

"We" are the Christian community who may have caused anyone who is gay or lesbian, bisexual or transsexual to believe they are not loved by God. We have judged you, told you that the hottest corners of hell are reserved for you, and have caused you to think that all Christians feel the same way. We don't! And neither does Jesus Christ himself.

As a Christian man myself, and the Senior Pastor of a large, thriving church in the Bay Area of California, I have watched Christians blast the gay community with anti-gay sentiments, statements, signs, books, articles, and a downright lack of Christ-like acceptance. We have made it difficult, if not impossible, for you to enter our churches or make you feel accepted or wanted.

However, I can't point the finger too much at my Christian brothers, for there was a time I was not tolerant, understanding, or sympathetic to the gay community. I too made snide comments and poked fun at people living the gay life in my sermons. I saw the gay lifestyle in the same genre of sins as murder and adultery, if not worse. I hurt people's feelings and caused some to even leave our church. I made sarcastic remarks and made them the brunt of some of my jokes. I am so sorry. Please forgive me. I do sincerely apologize.

I am not gay, nor have I ever struggled with gay tendencies. I am married (25 years) and have 3 children: two boys, 23 and 20, and a 16 year old daughter. I live in Northern California, in fact, only about 15 miles from San Francisco. I do preach against sin - sins of all kinds. I teach the Bible line upon line and don't skip over the tougher passages. When I preach or teach, I am speaking to myself first, then the rest of the congregation. The reason is, I am not a preacher of my own agenda, but only of God's Word.

When I say a preacher please let me define my terms for the sake of clarity and understanding. Whenever I say preacher (or pastor), I mean people who have been called by God (an inner knowing) to proclaim His Word, not their own! A preacher's sole job is to stand up and teach the Bible accurately, in easy to understand terminology, with clarity and conviction, making it applicable to every day life.

Paul the Apostle, who wrote half of the New Testament, talking about preachers, said, "Therefore since through God's mercy we have this ministry, we do not lose heart. Rather, we have renounced secret and shameful ways; we do not use deception, nor do we distort the Word of God. On the contrary, by setting forth the truth plainly we commend ourselves to every man's conscience in the sight of God (2 Corinthians 4:1-2). Let me explain what he was saying: Whenever anyone has been called by God to preach His Word, the Bible, it is not because they are worthy, but only by God's mercy did He choose them to proclaim His Word. They are never to use deception or distort God's word, but they are to teach it in a way that is easy to understand. Paul continues in verse 5 of that chapter saying, *"For we do not preach ourselves, but Jesus Christ as Lord, and ourselves as your servants for Jesus sake"*.

The message of the Bible is God's message, not man's. He has given the responsibility to men to preach and teach it accurately, without deception or distortion. Paul says again in 1 Corinthians 4:1, "So then, men ought to regard us (preachers) as servants of Christ and as those entrusted with the secret things of God. Now it is required that those who have been given a trust must prove faithful. And by the way, when we preach, or teach, we are to speak the Truth in Love" (Ephesians 4:15).

I pastor a relatively large, public church with over 2,000 people who call our church home. Some come from nearby, and others from as far away as 40 miles or more. Each week we may have as many as 50 first time visitors, people who have either driven by our church wanting to check us out, have been invited by a friend, or have seen us on television. They come from every walk of life you can imagine. We have people in our church who are millionaires and people who are on welfare. We have people who are African American, Caucasian, Asian, Hispanic, people from the Islands, Jewish, others from Hinduism, Islam, Catholicism, ex gang leaders, drug dealers, criminals, and even some who were raised goody-two-shoes It is the coolest church in the world to pastor.

However, the ones I have offended the most are the people in the gay community. I had little understanding and even less tolerance for them. As I matured and grew, I realized I was called by God to reach everyone, including gays, with the gospel (good news) of Jesus Christ. As I started to research more of the gay lifestyle, my heart began to change. I have become more compassionate towards people in the gay lifestyle, and also more understanding of where they are coming from. I have talked to many gay people concerning their struggles, and for many the struggle seems to be two-fold:

1) Dealing with so-called Christian conservatives, and other people who think like them, with their view of gay people;

2) The inner struggles gays themselves sometimes have being immersed in this lifestyle.

Of course, there are many gay people who don't struggle with either of these issues and are just living their life, not paying much attention to what the straight community says or how they feel. However, for many, there is a deep inner battle of feeling like, "this is just who I am." It is the way God made me. How can a loving God judge me for the way He made me?"

You may be saying right now, I'm gay, so what? Even if I wasn't born gay, who are you, or anyone else for that matter, to tell me what is right or wrong, or what is acceptable or not? You have a good point. That is why I have written this book. Who does have the right to tell someone else how they should live? Will you at least keep reading? I may have a point or two for you to consider. My heart especially goes out to those of you who were sexually abused when you were younger. This may have caused great confusion for you growing up and I will be addressing that issue more in Chapter 5 of this book.

Because most heterosexuals, Christian, or not, have little to no concept or understanding of what gays are talking about, they simply judge them as the worst of sinners. It wasn't until someone I knew very well shared with me the deep struggle he was having with knowing what God has said in His Word, and yet feeling he had no control over the fact that he was attracted to the same sex, that I began a deep study of this subject. It was at this point that I really began to understand some deeper truths of this lifestyle.

It is really from a stance of ignorance that most Christians approach the issue of judging all gays as terrible sinners. My desire in this book, Let's Get the Gay Thing Straight, is to help the Christian community see the gay community with new eyes - eyes of compassion - which the Lord himself has, and to help the gay community forgive us for our lack of Christ-likeness and really understand, maybe for the first time, what God's Word says about this issue. I hope to impart truth concerning all Jesus himself is saying to both parties. This will make some Christians mad, but before you prejudge, allow this preacher to finish his thoughts. I promise you, I will come from a scriptural standpoint, yet fully convey the heart of Christ to anyone in the gay lifestyle.

You may be a Christian, or you may be gay. Or you may call yourself a Christian and be gay! You may be a Christian and have friends who are involved in the gay lifestyle who don't want anything to do with your God. You may be gay, but privately, afraid you will be ostracized by your family or church. Maybe, just maybe, you secretly hate gay people and what they stand for. Or possibly, you are a Christian who openly condemns gay people and you may even feel right about it. It is also possible that many who read this book are neither Christian nor gay. All of you, just hang on. We will all learn something here!

If you have read this far, you might as well go ahead and finish the book. There is a reason you picked it up in the first place. If you approach this book with an open mind, I promise you will learn some things you previously didn't know. Dealing with people just about every day of my life, I realize that pride can stand in our way and keep us from exploring what we believe to be true, and that can be unfortunate for us. At least allow yourself to be open to the conversation. I believe you will get something out of it, in fact, I know you will. And even if you shouldn't change your stance, at least you will know the other side of the argument and what they are saying.

We are going to look at the practical side, the scientific side, the Biblical side, and the cultural side of this multifaceted topic. You will read things in the following chapters to which some will say, "Yea, that's right. Others might say, "What? Are you kidding me?" And I believe quite a few will say, "I didn't know that". So pull up a chair and let's continue.

CHAPTER
2

THE PATH LESS TRAVELED

"**Y**ou show me yours, I'll show you mine. No, you go first. You pull down your pants, then I'll pull down mine." Do you remember the first time you played this game? I'm sure you do. Every kid experienced a curiosity stage of what others looked like when we were growing up. We even did some things we knew were wrong, but our curiosity was simply stronger than our self control. So, they showed us what they had, and we showed them what we had. Some people may have been forced to show others what they had and yet, we all saw the private parts of others and they saw ours.

Before we get too far, I will be addressing multiple aspects of:

A) growing up gay,

B) growing up believing you were gay,

C) growing up straight and then becoming gay.

However, I will address each topic one at a time.

I grew up with only one brother and no sisters, in a solid Christian home in the Bay Area. Our family went to church a minimum of two nights a week, then on Sunday mornings, and sometimes again Sunday nights. My parents were old school. My dad was 50 when I was born and my mom was 40. They had lived through the depression and a couple of world wars. Sex was not talked about in our house, at least not until I was older and already sexually active.

In those early growing up years with my brother, from birth to about 7 or 8 years old, I had never seen what a girl looked like naked. I had no idea that girls were missing parts. Needless to say, the first time we played show and don't tell in my neighborhood, boy was I surprised! I stood there with my mouth wide open thinking, "There is something wrong with her. She don't look right."

At about age 17, I began to discuss with my Christian parents my anti-biblical stance of why I thought they were wrong concerning my girlfriend and I having sex. I reasoned that if my girlfriend and I loved each other, why couldn't we have sex? To me, my parents were wrong, narrow minded, and too Christian for me. Sex is what it was all about! They continued to tell me that sex was for marriage and that God was the one who created sex, and He should know what was best. They talked about sin, punishment, judgment, and how God knew everything I would ever do, no matter how secret I was about it. I simply did not agree.

So, what was really interesting about the show and don't tell days was, as a little boy or a little girl, you could become excited about someone else and how they looked naked, boy to boy or girl to girl. Because any kid could get excited or turned on by seeing the naked body of another, even if they were of the same sex, one could start down a path of attraction, and then say they have always liked the same sex. The fact of the matter is, a naked body of either sex can turn someone on at that age.

Sex is exciting, and there is something about the naked body when you see someone who may be sexually aroused or in a provocative position (like in a magazine or a video) that turns all of us on. This is why there is so much confusion on the subject of sex and our human sexuality. God ordained it to be enjoyed only within certain perimeters. Any man or woman can get excited while looking at nude pictures of another human being. Why do you think they make about $10 billion a year off the porn industry with magazines, videos, and the internet. Somebody is paying the money to look at that stuff. Human nakedness is usually a turn-on, especially when the picture or person you are looking at is aroused or in a sexually explicit posture. Sexual stuff arouses our sexual appetites and drives.

Remember, at that young age of 7-8, girls looked strange to me just because I was unfamiliar with how they really looked. After that very first time of seeing a girl naked, I remember thinking for a few years, that, not all girls could look like that, could they? The ones I saw must have been some kind of freaks or something. Boys were made right I reasoned, those girls were weird For a long time that thought consumed my thinking. Every time I saw a girl I would think, "She can't look like those other girls I saw, could she? But guess what, they all do! Missing parts and all!

In third grade, however, I had a crush on my teacher, Mrs. Warwick. She just looked pretty to me. I remember being mad when her husband picked her up one day from school and gave her a kiss! I wanted to punch him in the nose. I guess looking back, it was at this point that I thought girls and women were attractive. But confusion was coming.

At about age 11, I was developing into a pretty good athlete, especially baseball. I had thrown a four hit shut-out in the Oakland city championship at age 9, and played 3rd base and batted lead off in the city championship at age 11, and guess who was the starting left fielder? Ricky Henderson! It was at this time that I met an older teenage boy I will call Jeff Johnson. Jeff was a stud of an athlete. Curly blond hair, ripped abs and pecs, good looking and a total jock. In the summer, all the guys would play basketball at the local schoolyard. Us younger guys would play our own games, but whenever the older kids were playing, we would just watch. These guys were anywhere from five to eight years older and much bigger and stronger then us 11 and 12 year-olds, so we seldom, if ever, were able to play.

Because it was summer and usually hot outside, one team would play with shirts on and one with shirts off. At the half way point, they would switch. Whenever Jeff would play with his shirt off, I just thought he was the coolest guy. I mean, to me, he looked like how a guy should look. I admired his physique, his athletic ability, and his looks. It would have been very easy for someone to convince me that

I must like boys. But the reality was, I just admired him as an older guy. Had someone known that I thought Jeff was that cool, they might have tried to convince me that I must like the same sex. I didn't. I just wanted to be like him. In fact, now that I'm 52, I'm still in top shape. I have literally stayed in shape all my life because of Jeff's childhood influence. Of course I have admired the physiques of other men through the years and still can confidently say when another man carries himself with class, I think that is cool. But, I am not gay. To me, my wife is one sexy woman and that's the way it is!

This is what has happened to a lot of young boys growing up. At some point they may have had an admiration, quasi-attraction experience, and think back now saying, "I have always been attracted to the same sex". Not necessarily. Their first gay experience didn't mean that they were always gay. It is completely natural for all of us to admire other people, whether of the same sex or the opposite sex. And just because that may be true, that doesn't equal someone being gay.

I know what you are thinking:"As a gay man, I've never been attracted to females or, if a woman, "I have never been attracted to males, so how can you make that a definitive statement? Even if you say that you have never been attracted to a female (or a male), I would challenge your statement. For example, wasn't there a young girl whom you thought was cute, or pretty, or who got your attention when you were younger (females just reverse the analogy)? Even heterosexual women find other women attractive. If you said no, you may not be totally honest with yourself.

I just told you that as a heterosexual male, I have admired the looks of other men. That is a far cry from being gay. We are going to talk about other factors of being gay, such as growing up with feminine characteristics, playing with Barbies or other dolls well into grade school, being abused sexually by an older man, having a high pitched voice, or feeling more comfortable around the same sex than the opposite sex, but we will deal with them one at a time.

Generally speaking, yes usually, when a guy is gay, there has been a chain reaction of events in his life. He may have thought that other guys were cool or may have been molested by an older boy. Maybe he had a harsh or controlling mother, or a dad who seemed to favor the other kids, or was absent or harsh himself. Maybe as a young man he was exposed to a gay act, watched porn, or was hurt by a female. Take any one of these or more, coupled with having admired people of the same sex growing up, and now he is convinced he has always been this way. This is not necessarily true! Don't kid yourself. It is a fact that events and environment play a significant role in the shaping of who we are as adults.

Let's talk about young boys growing up with feminine characteristics. As an adolescent, maybe they had a high voice, liked playing with dolls, looked a little more feminine than the other boys, or liked hanging around older ladies. None of these, in and of themselves, equal being gay. That was just their makeup and personality. That does not equate being gay. You can think of a couple of star entertainers and professional boxers who had voices that sounded a little higher than the average guy's, but that didn't mean they were gay. Your orientation may have been towards the same sex but it doesn't equal being gay.

Usually, a young boy with feminine characteristics is teased by siblings, schoolmates, and neighborhood kids. That little boy begins to feel different, like maybe there is something wrong with him. The name calling and the unfair treatment by the other kids convince him that he must be different, so he begins to think that way. Over time, he finds like minded kids and they have a connection, a friendship. Once they get to the curiosity stage of show and don't tell, some deep seeded beliefs begin to develop. But again, that doesn't mean they were necessarily born that way. It just might surprise you that there is a story like this in the Bible. A story of two brothers.

THE TALE OF TWO BROTHERS

There is a story in the Bible of two brothers named Esau and Jacob. These boys were fraternal twins, not identical twins, which simply means they were born at the same time, but did not look exactly alike. Esau was born first and Jacob came out right on the heels of Esau. Jacob literally was holding on to the heel of his brother when he came out, and his name even means heel catcher (see Genesis 25: 24-26). Jacob's name was eventually changed to Israel (meaning both Prince of God, and One who struggles with God); he became the father of the nation of Israel.

The Bible says that he, Jacob (Israel), liked hanging around the tents with the women, learning to do stuff women like to do, while his older brother Esau was an outdoor kind of guy. Esau was a hairy man and a hunter. He was burly and liked being with the guys doing guy stuff. Jacob, on the other hand, had nice smooth skin, liked cooking, and had a gentle disposition. Which one do you think came out gay?

Neither!

They both had many wives and a bunch of kids! If Jacob had been accosted by a man sexually, or affected by any number of environmental influences, he might have turned out gay and he, and others, would have probably thought he was always that way. People would have said,"He was always such a sensitive and caring young boy. He enjoyed being around women and even had feminine characteristics. Besides, his dad favored his brother; we just knew he would be gay".

But Jacob was **not** gay. He was every bit a man's man as his brother Esau, even though he **was** wired differently. Now, you might say that it just wasn't accepted in that culture. Well, you are right, it wasn't. But it was accepted in every culture around him. What does that mean? What role does society and culture play in our different lifestyles? If it wasn't acceptable in his culture, and that prevented him from going gay, would he have been gay if he were raised in a different culture? If he were raised in a more gay friendly society and went over to the gay lifestyle, would that mean that he was always gay? Would that make it a predetermined biological make up, or a choice based on upbringing and culture?

Esau, his brother, probably looked something like Dick Butkus or Mike Ditka. I think the modern term is a Hegemonic man. A man's man: deep voice, mustache, athletic, doesn't cry, strong kind of guy. This type of guy looks like there isn't a feminine cell in their body. However, some gay men look and act this way, too. I know I am stereotyping here, but Esau clearly looked straight and we would have identified Jacob as, well, less macho, maybe.

EVENTS AND ENVIRONMENTS

In keeping with this story, culture had a huge influence on the sexual orientation of many of the people in their society. Remember, the nations all around Jacob, everywhere he went, were involved in very liberal sexual practices. I will show you just how diverse all the nations were in an upcoming chapter, and why. However, Jacob, who was in all respects much more feminine than his burly brother Esau, didn't cave in to the practices around him. But if he had, it would have been easy to say that he was born that way.

The fact is, Jacob had four wives and at least 13 children. Twelve of them were boys and these twelve became the Twelve Tribes of Israel. Just because he had smooth skin, liked to hang around the tents with the women, enjoyed cooking and probably interior decorating, didn't mean he was born with a gay gene. And remember, living not too far away were many people who practiced the gay lifestyle. He had every opportunity to swing that way if he wanted, but he didn't.

My point here is simply this: Just because you may have seemed more feminine (or Tom-boyish if a girl) than the other kids growing up, and just because you may have admired someone from the same sex when you were younger, does NOT mean you were gay. I believe other factors played a part. If today you claim that you are gay, and have always been this way, I want to challenge you to carefully rethink your life growing up.

Many gay men grew up in a straight environment and then turned to the gay life later. Since I have been a pastor for over 20 years now, I have seen some men who at one time attended our church during junior high and high school, who later took jobs in work places which were more gay-friendly, and after trying a gay experience switched all the way over to the gay lifestyle. I have been told that many areas of dance, theater, music and modeling (these are just a few) can be hotbeds for the gay community to desire to work in. I am not at all saying that everyone who works in these fields is gay, or that gay people only seek work in these fields. There are gay people in every strata of life, including the priesthood and more recently, the pulpit!

What I am saying is, if people place themselves in a gay environment, it is quite possible that at some point they might try the gay thing and never turn back to the straight. They might say at that point that they were always gay, but I would question their statement. In upcoming chapters we will look at the scientific data concerning the reality of a gay gene. But if there is no gay gene there has to be an explanation for their sexual preference. If we are to say that people are born gay with a gay gene, and therefore it is just the way they are, God has some explaining to do and I really don't have anything more to say. But, if there is no gay gene then we can have an intelligent conversation.

But what if there is not scientific proof at all? What if in fact, just the opposite is true? If that is the case, then, like Ricky Ricardo used to say, "Lucy, you got some 'splaining' to do".

So, please continue reading...you might be surprised!

CHAPTER
3

IS THERE SCIENTIFIC PROOF?

When someone is looking for scientific proof that people are born gay, or that they have a gay gene which predisposes them towards the gay lifestyle, it is almost like putting a gun to a scientist's head and saying, "You better prove to them that gay people are born this way. In other words, they had better come up with proof that this is true or else. But what if scientifically there isn't any proof? What if the data just doesn't match up? What if it is proven scientifically, as well as from the Bible, that this simply is not the case? Would that change the sexual behavior of people? Maybe, but probably not.

In a study done by Swedish scientists on measuring the brain sizes of gay men and heterosexual women, they said that, the left half of their brain was of similar size, while the right side was bigger in lesbian women and heterosexual men. Said one UK scientist, "This was evidence that sexual orientation was set in the womb."[1]

Did you catch that? This was evidence that sexual orientation was set in the womb? Really?

The report states: Scientist have noticed for some time that homosexual people of both sexes have differences in certain cognitive abilities, suggesting there may be subtle differences in their brain structure. This is the first time, however, that scientists have used brain scanners to try to look for the source of those differences. A group of 90 healthy gay and heterosexual adults, men and women, were scanned by the Karolinska Institute scientists to measure the volume of both sides, or hemispheres of the brain.[2]

When the results were collected, it was found that lesbians and heterosexual men shared a particular asymmetry in their hemisphere size,while heterosexual women and gay men had no difference between the size of the different halves of their brain. The conclusion by Dr. Qazi Rahman, from the University of London was, "As far as I'm concerned there is no argument anymore if you are gay, you are born gay."[3]

Did you get that? From that study of just 90 people who have similar half brain sizes, proves people are born gay? Wow, now that's some scientific proof! Was he serious? I would be open to the scientific proof, if there was any...I just haven't seen it yet. I think that you would like to know the truth, too. There has to be some more conclusive scientific study and research to hang our hats on than that.

But because I know you want to know what science says, I did some research for you. Of course, I would like you to do your own as well, but for now here are some of the forensic studies which have been done. Dr. Neil Whitehead Ph.D has also done research on identical twins.

"There have been two major published registry studies, one based on the Minnesota registry and the other on the Australian registry. The larger of the two registry studies is the Australian one, done by Bailey, Martin and others at the university of Queensland. Using the 14,000+ Australian twin collection, they found that if one twin was homosexual, 38% of the time the other one was too. For lesbians the concordance was 30%. Whether 30% or 38 %, all the studies agree, it is clearly not 100%."[4]

What does that mean? If the twins are identical in every way, then they should also be the same in their sexual orientation, and this just simply is not the case! Whitehead goes on to say, "The critical factor is that if one identical twin is homosexual, only sometimes is the co-twin homosexual. There is no argument about this in the scientific community."[5] Did you get that? There is no argument about this in the scientific community! Let me continue with the Doctor's findings.

Identical twins have identical genes. "If homosexuality was a biological condition produced inescapably by the genes, then if one identical twin was homosexual, in 100% of the cases his brother would be too. But we know that only about 38% of the time is the identical twin brother homosexual. Genes...do not force people into homosexuality. This conclusion has been well known in the scientific community for a few decades but has not reached the general public. Indeed, the public increasingly believes the opposite."[6]

Now, that is interesting, isn't it? The scientific community has known the truth for decades but the public has been made to believe something different. Whitehead continues:

Identical twins had essentially the same upbringing. Suppose homosexuality resulted from some interaction with parents that infallibly made children homosexual. Then if one twin was homosexual, the other would also be homosexual. But as we saw above, if one is homosexual, the other is usually not. Family factors may be an influence, but on the average do not compel people to be homosexual. Twin studies suggest that as a class, events unique to each twin, are more frequent than genetic or family influences.

But many individual family factors (such as a distant father) are more common than the individual unique factors. Unique events would include seduction, sexual abuse, chance sexual encounters, or particular reactions to sensitive events, when young. Everyone has their own unique path which only partly follows that of the theoreticians.[7]

If I may, I'll try to simplify what he is saying: If homosexual behavior were simply a by-product of our genetic make up, then it would be true 100%, or nearly 100% of the time. However, the scientific research does not reveal this as a fact. Instead, according to Whitehead, identical twins with identical genetic makeups, differ in their sexual proclivities. He is also saying that the evidence points to events which took place in the child's life and how they individually responded to these, and this was the biggest factor in someone being homosexual.

Before I unfold further research for you, let me state right here that if genetics played the major role in someone being homosexual, then God would have a lot of explaining to do concerning judging someone for their sexual sin. It wouldn't be fair, now would it? If God made someone this way, how can He then tell them they shouldn't be that way? But, scientific proof doesn't support the notion or hypothesis that people are born this way.

It would be fair to say then, that someone who was prone to drinking is so because of their genetic code. We can get really crazy and say that people all do what they do because of how their parents' genes combined to make them who they are. This line of reasoning would then give everyone an excuse for doing what they do. If that were the case, how would anyone be responsible for how they behave? Everyone would just be living out their basic God-given traits. I don't think you really believe that, do you?

In another study of identical twins, there was a higher concordance percentage of both twins being gay. However, allow me to highlight the discrepancies stated in *Exploring the Dimensions of Human Sexuality* (Fourth Ed), a textbook used in academia today. According to their reports, the one most frequently cited is the study done by Kallman (1952). His particular study was also done on both identical and fraternal twins. Consequently, the environments are the same for both sets of twins, but the difference is genetic makeup.

Kallman found identical twins had a 95% concordance rate (both twins were homosexual) compared to a 12% concordance rate for fraternal twins. He concluded that homosexuality is a function of genetic disposition. Whitman and Diamond (1986) reported a concordance rate of 75% for identical twins and a 19% rate for fraternal twins, thereby supporting the genetic theory. However, numerous other studies over the years (Heston and Shields, 1968; Zuger, 1976) have not been able to verify Kallman's findings.[8]

It is amazing to me that when these so-called findings for the proof of genetic makeup are investigated, they don't stand up to scrutiny. Within the scientific community there is no verifiable proof for there being a gene that causes people to be gay.

Additional research also finds discrepancies in this argument:

Bailey and Pillard (1991) also studied twins. They looked at identical twins, fraternal twins, and adopted brothers, among whom one of each pair had declared himself to be homosexual. They found that the more genetically similar each was to his gay brother, the more likely he was to be gay as well. Homosexuality was found in the remaining member of each pair in 52% of the identical twins (who developed from the same ovum), 22% of the fraternal twins (who developed from different ova), and only 11% of the adopted brothers (who shared no common genetic material).[9]

"The researchers estimated that between 30% and 70% of the determining factors of homosexuality are genetic. However, questions remain: Even if 70% is genetic, what accounts for the other 30%? What role do prenatal hormonal secretions play? What role does environment play once the child is born? *"Sexuality experts do caution that a specific gene linked to homosexuality has not been identified"* (p. 360-361, emphasis added). Let me quote that again: Sexuality experts do caution that a specific gene linked to homosexuality has not been identified.

I could go on and on. But I think you get the point; there is no scientific proof which can be verified concerning a so-called gay gene. It simply doesn't exist. However, that doesn't mean, based on a multiplicity of factors, that some people will not end up gay or bisexual or lesbian. I just want us to be clear that we were not born that way. And whether it was because of sexual abuse, an overbearing mother or an absentee father, a bad heterosexual relationship, curious sexual encounters, a decision based solely on someone's preference or choice, or simply getting caught up in the sex whirlpool. Jesus of Nazareth wants to bring healing and freedom back to our lives. He is not trying to take away our fun but rather to help us live the kind of wholesome lives He, God, wants us to live.

Please let me continue with more research from the scientific field. Again, I emphasize why I'm giving you these findings: If it can be proven that there is a gay gene God would have some explaining to do (and quite honestly, I would have very little to say, if anything at all). However, if there is not a biological reason for one being gay, we can at least have critical dialogue on the topic.

Dr. Dean Hamer was asked by Scientific American if homosexuality was rooted solely in biology. Hamer replied: "Absolutely not. From twin studies we already know that half or more of the variability in sexual orientation is not inherited. Our studies try to pinpoint the genetic factors, not negate the psychosocial factors...Homosexuality is not purely genetic. Environmental factors play a role. There is not a single master gene that makes people gay. I don't think that we will ever be able to predict who will be gay".[10]

So, why do people do what they do? Because we all have a sin gene, or what we call a sin nature, if you would. It's not that we human beings can't do good things, or things that are right, because we do all the time. Rather, it's that we can't help doing what is wrong! The Bible says, "The things I want to do, I don't do, and the things I don't want to do, I do. Therefore, it is no longer I who do it, but sin living in me" (Rom 7:15-16).

Did you get that? It is sin living in me! That is the "**GENE** everyone possesses. Including me and you. A SIN GENE! BUT IT IS A SPIRITUAL GENE, NOT A PHYSIOLOGICAL ONE.

Dr. Whitehead finalizes his research by saying:

The scientific truth is our genes don't force us into anything. But we can support or suppress our genetic tendencies. We can foster them or foil them. If we reinforce our genetic tendencies thousands of times (even if only through homo-erotic fantasy), is it surprising that it is hard to change? Similarly, we have a genetic tendency to eat, but it is possible to foster this tendency and overeat for the pleasure it brings. If we repeat that often enough, we will not only reinforce a genetic tendency to become overweight, but find that starving the habit takes a long time![11]

What is he saying? Simply, that anything we as human beings become mentally obsessed with and then put into practice, will become a habit of life. It will become more and more difficult to break the habit the longer we let it consume our thinking and practice it as a behavior. This is true with anything in life for any human being, Christian, non christian, gay or straight, we are creatures of habits and pleasures, and we are slaves to whatever revolves in our minds. Think about it, what is it that you constantly think about? It's O.K. Go ahead and be honest, at least with yourself.

The Word of God, the Bible, says the same thing. It says that, "a man is a slave to whatever masters him" (2 Peter 2:20). It also says that, "we are to take captive (or control) every thought unto the obedience of Christ" (2 Corinthians 10:4). Philippians 4:8 says, "Think on these things; whatever is true, whatever is noble, whatever is right, whatever is pure, whatever is lovely, whatever is admirable... think on these things."

In the Sermon on the Mount, which I will elaborate on in further in the next chapter, Jesus talked about lusting other people sexually (by the way, to look lustfully means to stare with a deep sexual longing). The reason he talked about this issue was because the people in that society would pride themselves that they hadn't physically slept with someone other than their spouse, but every time a woman walked by, the men would stare with little to no self control. Jesus, like He always does, got to the heart of the matter. In other words He was saying, **"Just because you haven't or can't sleep with other people, doesn't mean you still aren't committing sin with them in your heart"**. This includes lusting after the same sex or after the opposite sex. Sex, any kind of sex, with a person to whom you are not married, is sin. Plain and simple! This is God's standard and many people don't like it. Why? Because we don't want anyone governing our lives, including and especially God!

If there is no gay gene, and being gay is simply a choice one makes based on whatever reason they want to base it on, and with that, if there is a God and the Bible is His Word and His Word says that sexual sin is defined as any sex outside of marriage, that puts people in a difficult place of having to make some decisions. The easier thing for them to do is say there is no God, or that the Bible is written by men and therefore can't be trusted, or that God Himself made me this way, therefore how can He judge me for it. Otherwise, the only other option people have is to acknowledge that it is a sin, and now they have to do something about it. So, which is it? Well, let's look at some more facts, both scientific and Biblical.

CHAPTER
4

WHAT WOULD
JESUS SAY?

If Jesus were walking the earth today, what do you think he would say to the gay community? Would he even visit them? Remember, Jesus came to seek and save the lost (Luke 19:10). He went to where the sinful folks lived. He had lunch with prostitutes and criminals, with drunkards and tax collectors. He even went to the religious centers and paid them a visit. He left no one out. He said to all of them, "All that the Father (God) gives to me will come to me, and whoever comes to me I will never drive away" (John 6:37). So, would he have gone to the gay community? Would he have even considered them sinful?

YOUR ANSWER IS IMPORTANT

Your answer is important, because if Jesus did go to the gay community, that would mean they were sinners, too. Now, if homosexuality isn't a sin, Jesus still would have visited that community to tell them about The Kingdom of Heaven. Remember, He didn't come to call the righteous, but sinners to repentance (Luke 5:32). Now, we know that all of us are sinners, and if the gay life is not sin, then what sins would Jesus have addressed in the gay community? If Jesus were OK with homosexuality, and yet still went to see them, what sin would He be trying to turn them from? Interesting thought, to say the least.

You might say, "Well, Jesus would have talked to them about other issues of life. Stuff all of us deal with. Things like treating people right, keeping your word, being honest, helping the poor, etc". O.K. You are right. But there was probably a host of other things He would have talked about, as well. Whenever Jesus talked about sexual sins, He used the Greek word pornia. It is where we get the word pornography from. This word indicated any and all types of sexual sin.

Jesus identified with all humanity. He was equally comfortable with the rich, the poor, the sick and diseased, the outcasts, and the so called religious. We know this because He visited them all. Why would He do that? Why would He go to every group in the social strata? Was the point to not leave anyone out? Or was it because He knew that every person needed to hear about His Father's love and mercy, His laws for living, and about His judgment and His grace?

In Matthew 9:36 it says that, **When he (Jesus) saw the crowds, he had compassion on them, because they were harassed and helpless, like sheep without a shepherd.** He saw everyone in need of His grace, mercy, power and help. But it wasn't just their physical needs that He was concerned about. Inasmuch as He was concerned about those daily and physical needs, it wasn't just that. He cared about their pain, brokenness, sin, and their bondage to things in life which God wanted to set them free from. He wanted to also tell them of his Father's love. He wanted them to know that even though no one could measure up to His Father's standards, His Father had sent him (Jesus) to tell the people of the grace and forgiveness which was now available to them. The standard the Father (God) had set for people to live by was unobtainable for every human being. His laws were too holy. The flesh is too weak. Temptation is too strong, and mankind as a whole had completely turned their backs on him. "There is none righteous, not even one"! (Romans 3:10, exclamation added).

Jesus demonstrated this in the Sermon on the Mount

I have been to the supposed site of this incredible sermon, called the Sermon on the Mount. This sermon is also known as the Beatitudes. It comes from a Latin word meaning happy, or blissful. This means you are blessed or will be happy if you do them. A quick look at them will shed some light on what Jesus was trying to say. The Bible says there were thousands of people present when he first shared this sermon. Some have called it the greatest sermon ever preached.

Jesus said, "You have heard that it was said, 'Do not commit murder, and anyone who murders will be subject to judgment'. But I tell you, that anyone who is angry with his brother (another person), will be subject to judgment" (Matt 5:21-22). Everyone of us has done that. I know I have been mad at others in my heart before. How about you? When He said, "You have heard it said", He meant this is what the religious teachers have taught you. The people had heard the religious teachers say "Do not commit murder", but with this deeper definition of being angry in your heart at someone, who hasn't committed murder?

'Subject to judgment' meant the verdict of the court for capital punishment under Jewish law. Jesus was saying that it isn't just the physical act of murder God is looking at, but rather, what is going on in the human heart that will expose a person to God's standard of judgment. Jesus goes on to say, **"You have heard it said** (again, what the teachers had taught the people) **'Thou shalt not commit adultery'. But I tell you, that anyone who looks at a woman (or a man) lustfully has already committed adultery with them in his heart** (Matt 5:27-28). All of us have done that, too. No one is exempt. What He was trying to show us was that every human being falls short of God's glory, or His Holiness. We are all sinners. Straight and gay. Rich and poor. Black, white, red, yellow, or brown, it doesn't matter. Jesus had come to call everyone to repent. He was showing them the way to salvation.

It seems that some Christians have forgotten that they too were once outside God's perfect plan for humanity. They seem to forget that God called each one of us who are now Christians out of our sinful lives to both live for Him and to tell others about His love and grace. Instead, we have become the judge and the jury of everyone else's life and lifestyle.

Jesus said later in Matt 7:1-2, "Do not judge, or you too will be judged. For in the same way you judge others, you will be judged... Why do you look at the speck of sawdust in your brother's eye and pay no attention to the plank in your own eye"? Paul later said in 1 Corinthians 5:12-13, "What business is it of mine to judge those outside the church? Are you not to judge those inside the church? God will judge those outside."

Yes, as a Christian and as a preacher, I am called to tell people what God's Word says about sin. Yes, I am to try to turn sinners from the error of their ways. Yes, if something is not right by God's standards I am to speak up for what is right in God's eyes. But the way the Christian community has gone about this is WRONG!

To make matters worse, we have categorized sins. We say some are worse than others. Some would say to tell a white lie isn't the same as murder, or that cussing isn't the same as adultery. In one sense this is true and in another it isn't. Yes, murder is one of the worst things anyone could do. It is one of the ten commandments. "Thou shalt not murder" (Exodus 20:13). To take the life of another human being is the worst of sins. God himself said in Genesis 9:5-6, "And for your lifeblood I will surely demand an accounting. I will demand an accounting from every animal. And from each man, too, I will demand an accounting for the life of his fellowman. Whoever sheds the blood of man, by man shall his blood be shed; for in the image of God has God made man. However, lying is also breaking one of the ten commandments. "Thou shalt not lie" (Exodus 20:16).

James, the Lord's brother, wrote one of the books in the Bible and in it he said, "If you break one of the commandments, you have broken them all" (James 2:8-11). That means whether you have lied, stolen, committed murder, or adultery, if you have taken God's name in vain, or coveted (desired) what someone else has, all of these are classified as sin. Each and every one of them is an affront to God. Each and every one of us has committed some, if not all of them.

We have all heard the news of people being murdered and have imagined what the family must go through. As a Pastor, I have counseled dozens of families who have suffered through this unimaginable loss and needless waste of life. Maybe you have experienced it firsthand yourself. If so, you know better than I the painful aftermath of an atrocity of this magnitude.

I have also watched the devastating effects of adultery and the deep pain it has caused entire families, including the innocent children. Although many families have been able to rebound from these situations, it is a long and painful process. This is why God commanded us to not violate His holy and righteous laws. If we do, we will destroy each other.

Sin is sin. Period! Remember why God gave these commands. It was out of His mercy and love for us that He presented His laws to us. He was trying to help us so we wouldn't destroy each other. We know that the human heart can be a wicked thing, even when we put on a mask to hide our true motives and our true selves. We are capable of pride, greed, slander, gossip, arrogance, rebellion, addiction, revenge, and infidelity. We can be cutthroat, backbiting, and calloused. Need I continue?

How about selfish, insecure, rude, unfair, and downright hostile. I think you are getting the point.

What God was trying to tell us was that if you treat each other this way, it will break down society. One way to look at the Ten Commandments is to see it as two categories. The first four commands have to do with us loving God. Keep a mental note of how many and how often we break these laws.

THE TEN COMMANDMENTS:

1) Have no other God besides me.

2) Don't make an idol of anything and call it God.

3) Do not use my name in vain (curse using His name, or saying "Oh my God etc".).

4) Keep the sabbath day Holy.

How are you doing so far? The first four commandments have to do with how we behave towards God. The next six commandments have to do with how we treat each others as humans beings:

5) Honor your father and mother.

6) Do not murder.

7) Do not commit adultery.

8) Do not steal.

9) Do not lie.

10) Do not covet (want what someone else has; i.e. wife, husband, car, house, clothes, etc).

You see, if we violate these laws, society will destroy itself. What happens when a C.E.O. steals from the company? Not only do stocks drop, but trust in the company is depleted, and team morale sinks to an all time low. Others in the company may follow this example, no longer caring for the good of the company. What about the family of the perpetrator? The embarrassment of the wife and kids, family and friends? The list goes on and on.

As we said, the first four commands have to do with loving God. God continues His commands by talking about our children. He says, "Children, obey your parents". If children don't obey their parents, anarchy will run rampant. It is common knowledge that if a child doesn't respect or listen to his parents, there is no one in society they will listen to. God continued by saying "If you murder each other, you will destroy each other. If you commit adultery, you will destroy families. If you steal...." you get the point.

Yes, even though not all sins have the same effect as others, sin is destructive to ourselves, our families, and our societies. And Jesus came to save sinners. All of them. That is why, we as Christians, have not properly represented Christ to the gay community. We have made them out to be the most vile of sinners. We have looked down our righteous noses and have pointed our ten foot fingers in their faces and have told them: **TURN OR BURN!**

My belief is that Jesus would have come into the gay community, sat down with them and told them earthly stories to make heavenly points. These stories are called parables. A parable is an illustration people can understand and relate to - an earthly story with a heavenly principle. You would have heard the compassion in His voice and have seen the love in His eyes. You would have been drawn to His grace and would have deeply thanked Him for having healed a friend who may have been dying of cancer or of AIDS.

Let me give you a couple of illustrations from scripture. In John's gospel, chapter 8, there is a story of a woman caught in adultery. She is brought to Jesus and is accused of being caught in the very act! *(I wonder why they didn't bring in the man involved?)* Anyway, they said to Jesus, "Teacher, this woman was caught in the act of adultery. In the law (The Jewish law of adultery) Moses commanded us to stone such women. (That doesn't mean roll up a joint and get her high, it means to pick up rocks and throw them at her until she is dead). Now, what do you say?" (vs.5). They wanted to know what Jesus would say, because He was always hanging out with sinners and having mercy and grace on them. They wanted to see if he really was from God, because God would never violate His own law, and His law said stone adulterers.

After bending down and writing on the ground, then Jesus stood up and said, "If anyone is without sin, let him be the first to throw a stone" (vs. 7). With the oldest man leading the way, one by one, each of them dropped his stone and walked away. There was nothing anyone could say. Why? Because every one of us is a sinner. None of us could have stood before Jesus then or now! Then Jesus said to the woman, "Woman, where are they? Has no one condemned you"? (vs. 10). She said, "No one, sir," she said. Jesus said, **"THEN NEITHER DO I CONDEMN YOU. GO NOW, AND LEAVE YOUR LIFE OF SIN"** (vs. 11).

You see, Jesus forgave her. He had mercy and grace on her. He was moved with compassion towards her, but He did not leave her that way. He told her to change her life. He didn't ask her about her childhood. He didn't say "I know why you do this. It was because you were abused as a child or, I know your dad wasn't there for you growing up and it really affected you". Even if all those things were true in her life, and they may have been, Jesus simply forgave her and told her to live a new life. In essence, what He was saying was, "Now that you have experienced forgiveness and mercy, stop what you are doing and begin to live in a way that is pleasing to God".

Later in the New Testament, Paul said in Titus 2:11-13, "The grace of God that brings salvation has appeared to all men. It teaches us to say no to ungodliness and worldly passions, and to live self controlled, upright, and godly lives in this present age, while we wait for the blessed hope the glorious appearing of our great God and savior Jesus Christ".

What Paul was saying was, the only way to get saved is through God's grace. Grace defined means receiving something we don't deserve. When we accept God's grace and understand His love and kindness in giving it to us, we respond out of love in return and begin to change the way we live.

Let me give you another story in the Bible. Almost everyone has heard of Mary Magdalene. She became both a follower of Jesus and a very dear friend to him. Despite all the fiction that has been propagated about Jesus either having an affair with her or the two of them being married and having children, the Bible knows no such nonsense. What is remarkable is that Jesus had great plans for her life, even though at one time she had seven demons living inside her. Did you get that? Seven! (See Luke 8:1-3).

In that area of the world at that time, demon possession was real and common. In fact, Jesus spent considerable time helping people who were demon possessed. He would speak to the demon possessing the person and tell it to leave, and with just a simple command, the demons would flee. Sometimes he would lay hands on the person and the demon would come out. Can you believe that Mary had seven different demons in her?

Yet, after Jesus drove the demons out of Mary Magdalene by His power, she was so grateful that she became a devout follower of the Lord. She, along with a group of other women, helped to support him financially as well (Luke 8:3). On one occasion, she came into a house where Jesus was eating and brought a bottle of very expensive perfume, broke it, poured it on his feet, and wiped his feet with her hair (John 12:1-11). Amazing! All this from a woman who had been possessed by demons.

You see, she was responding to the grace Jesus had shown her. It literally changed her life. His grace and forgiveness was so astounding to her, that for the rest of her life she would follow her Lord. She was even the first at the grave site on the third day when Jesus rose from the dead. Once you have come face to face with God's grace, it has the power to change your whole direction in life, if you let it. It doesn't mean a job or career change (although it could), but an internal YOU change.

You probably don't have a demon inside you, at least I hope not, but God wants to turn your life around no matter what you have been involved in. He wants to bless you and use your life for His glory. Can you get with that? So many people have never tapped into the love God has for them. I can honestly tell you, it is the sweetest thing on earth!

All that to say, Christ came and displayed the great mercy of God, His Father, and we Christians have not been Christlike in our attitudes, words, conduct, or behavior towards the gay community. But in addition, the people Jesus showed his mercy to, also changed the way they were living. Both camps, Christians and gays, need to learn from the Lord Jesus. That is the point of this book.

CHAPTER
5

THE MODERN DAY
SEX REVOLUTION

HOW DID AMERICA BECOME
SO LOOSE IN ITS MORALS?

Even though there has always been sexual sin in America, 50 years ago it was much more discreet and covert in many areas of our country. The sexual revolution which began in the 1960's, actually started before the 1960's, and in part, came as a result of some research which was done by a Mr. Alfred Kinsey. Kinsey's findings sparked an interest in human sexuality which America will never turn back from.

The things which are openly tolerated today on television, at the movies, adult stores, Las Vegas, and now the biggest exposure - the Internet - have taken this country by storm. I would like to believe that you are aware of what is happening in America concerning the freedoms we practice in the sexual arena that are not good for this country. Come on, be honest with yourself. Do you really think this is what God had in mind?

Consider, if you would, that 12 and 13 year old girls are having to deal with their sexuality just to fit in with the other kids. As I write this, my own daughter has just turned 15, and there is no way she is ready to start engaging in that stuff. I know she knows about it, and I know all her friends talk about it. I also know that she and her girlfriends are half boy crazy, but to allow her to get involved with boys at this age *sexually* what kind of a father would I be? Really? I mean, is she ready to have a baby if she were to get pregnant? She can't even clean her room half the time, let alone care for a baby. You may say, "What if she practiced safe sex? Are you really serious? You and I - as adults - know that sometimes in the heat of passion we temporarily lose our minds, and it only takes one time of unprotected sex to get pregnant.

In addition, you know that guys sometimes don't want to use protection while having sex. If your argument is that she could have an abortion if she got pregnant, is she any more prepared for that? Would I want my daughter to go through the trauma and emotional pain that an abortion brings just because some boy wanted to have his way with her? Are you kidding me? There is a time, a place, and a purpose for sex, and age 15 ain't it!

So how did America fall into this freedom of what we call the sexual revolution? As already stated, the 60's opened the door to the liberality we now practice and hold to concerning sexuality in this country. It is not going away. Sex is too strong, too powerful, and we as humans are too weak and our habits of pleasure seeking are too accessible. I deal with people every day as a pastor and I hear the real life issues people struggle with; sex is one of the biggest issues, if not the biggest.

Based on the first two books I have written, Be A Man, and The Beauty of A Woman, I teach conferences all around this country. At these conferences, one of the sessions I always teach for men is about pornography and sexual sin. "Why," you might ask? Because, even though most of these men are Christians and claim to love God and know His Word concerning sexual sin, the vast majority of them are struggling with self control at some level. I have yet to meet a group of guys who, after I was done speaking said, "We don't struggle with this. Pastor, you wasted your time talking about that subject (sex); it doesn't concern us". Rather, it is just the opposite. I am met by man after man who is trying to make sense out of the struggle between knowing and wanting to do what is right, and never quite being able to do it. America has been sold a bill of goods and we have been paying for it as a nation ever since. Jesus said that Satan is a liar, and the father of lies (John 8:44). That means that every time he opens his mouth, he is lying! And he has lied to us in America about our sexuality.

James Boice (1979) compiled research in his commentary on the book of Genesis and, in part, about man's attempt to justify sin. Boice writes that in 1928, "Margaret Mead, the renowned anthropologist, wrote a book entitled <u>Coming of Age in Samoa</u>. This book was also used to justify and promote the so-called sexual revolution of the sixties. Ms. Mead, having arrived in Samoa in 1925 as a Columbia University student at the ripe old age of 23, spent the next two and a half months first learning the language. She made a study out of the lifestyle and behavior of Samoan adolescent females. She worked with 68 girls, however, the bulk of her data came from only 25 of them who frequently came and reported to her their sexual escapades from the night before."[12]

Somehow, this convinced Mead that the terrible teenage years were not a problem in Samoa, which she said, was due to the island's supposed sexual freedom. 'Free love promotes nonviolence' was her conclusion."[13] But, this data was later to be challenged. People back in the United States seemingly wanted to hear a report like this, of course, and her book soon became a classic. Fortunately, there were those who questioned the legitimacy of her findings.

Derek Freeman, an Australian anthropologist writing for Harvard University Press (Margaret Mead and Samoa: (The Making and Unmaking of an Anthropological Myth), has charged: "1) sex out of wedlock was illegal at the time of Mead's research, not accepted, as Mead claimed; 2) Samoan society has always been competitive, not relaxed and easygoing, as she stated; and 3) psychological disturbances like hysteria and compulsive behavior are commonplace, giving rise to high rates of assault, homicide, and rape, which Mead denied."[14]

It shocks me to see the inaccuracies in these research papers, yet they were presented as truth. Boice adds: "George Leonard used his position as senior editor of *Look* magazine to promote the sexual revolution during the 1960s. In 1970 he wrote, 'A society that considers most good feelings immoral and bad feelings moral perpetuates the ultimate human heresy: an insult, and if you will, to God and his works' ''. But today Leonard has changed his tune. In a 1983 publication, The End of Sex, he argued that the sexual revolution has not done what its proponents claimed it was doing. It has not enhanced sex; instead, it has only cheapened love.[15]

Let me state again for clarification: Sex is a good thing, and a God thing!!! He designed it for our pleasure. Sex was to be between a man and a woman who were committed for life in a loving and serving relationship with one another. Sex was God's design for mankind to continue producing and replenishing the human race. God had to make our sex drive strong so that we would want to come together sexually to reproduce and fill the earth (Genesis 1:28). God wanted a populated world where people work together and serve Him as the creator of everything.

But remember, everything God had made which was good and for a purpose, the devil and fallen humanity has perverted and twisted. Sex was never meant to be a 'free-for-all'. It was meant for two committed people to enjoy how and when they wanted; it was to be a private affair between the two of them.

So what happened? A man by the name of Alfred Kinsey, born in Hoboken, New Jersey, on June 23, 1894, and educated at Bowdoin College, who then received his Doctorate from Harvard University in Zoology, was known for his work on gall wasps. His work received renowned attention all throughout his field. However, it was while teaching a marriage class and being asked questions regarding sexual practices, that his interest in the study of human sexual behavior was first piqued. He set a long range goal of doing research on the sexual practices of humans, and the campus at Indiana University became a center for research in human sexual behavior.

Kinsey began his studies in 1938 in writing a progress report from a case study on human sexual behavior. By the time of his death in 1956, he had written two books, Sexual Behavior in the Human Male, which he completed in 1948, selling 300,000 copies, and in 1953, the sequel, Sexual Behavior in the Human Female, which sold 227,000 copies. That may not seem like a lot in today's culture, but it was pretty impressive back in the late 1940's and 50's.

Kinsey was responsible for bringing case studies of controversial subject matter out in the open for informed study. In his book the Sexual Behavior of the Human Female, he brought out findings in pre-adolescent, premarital, and extramarital relations among women. Many of his findings showed that what was considered normal sexual behavior, wasn't exactly what was being practiced behind closed doors.

Normal sexual behavior would be defined as husband/wife relations in private, just between the two of them. What Kinsey and his team found was that many people were dealing with sexual expressions beyond what was thought to be normal, but included masturbation, pedophilia, bisexuality, and homosexuality, just to name a few. Sex had always been a hush-hush topic, but now with his reports going public in book form, the American public began to say, "If it's okay for them, then it's okay for me too".

As other writers and talk shows began to disagree with him, this only brought more attention to the subject. Kinsey even made the cover of Time magazine, August 24, 1953. His articles also appeared in Life, Look, and McCall's magazines. The problem was not that he was simply making facts known the real issue was that many Americans saw this new unveiling of sexuality as a license for free sex in their own lives. No longer would the church and God's Word be the standard of morality for right and wrong.

The confusion lies in the fact that, although Kinsey was supposedly uncovering the naked truth of human sex practices which were being done in private, he failed to mention that almost all these practices (which were outside of God's intended purpose) were sinful and destructive to a society. No one stopped to see whether his research was honest, or valid, or exhaustive.

For example: Kinsey wrote about observations of orgasms in over three-hundred children between the ages of five months and fourteen years. This information was said to have come from adult - childhood memories or from parent or teacher observation. Kinsey also interviewed nine men who had sexual experiences with children.[16]

Did you get that, **with children**?!? What would we call that today? With children? Go ahead, tell me.

Needless to say, very little attention was paid to this part of Kinsey's research at the time, but where Kinsey had gained this information began to be questioned some 40 years later. It was later revealed that Kinsey used data from a single pedophile and presented it as being from various sources."[17]

Basically, he found a man who was abusing a little child and related the child's reaction during the abuse and called it a report saying this was his research from multiple investigations. Listen, if you study the behaviors of bank robbers, and psychologically walk through their every move, young bank robbers will learn better techniques on how to rob banks, but that will never make robbing banks right!

Kinsey may have even told the truth in some of his studies, but he is telling the truth about human sexual behavior that has migrated outside the boundaries of what was originally intended by the creator of sex; God!

James Jones wrote in 1997 in the biography <u>Alfred C. Kinsey: A Public/Private Life</u>, that Kinsey's own sexual activity influenced his work, that he over-represented prisoners and prostitutes, classified some single people as married, and that he included a disproportionate number of homosexual men, particularly from Indiana, in his sample, which may have distorted his studies...he also omitted African Americans from his studies."[18]

What was the effect of Kinsey going public with the wide variety of sexual behaviors found in sinful humanity? Let me put it this way, "Dad, everyone else is doing it, even the Johnsons down the street behave this way, so why can't I"? (How many times have our kids used that logic on us?)

Time magazine said concerning Kinsey's first book, "Not since 'Gone With the Wind' had booksellers seen anything like it."[19] His reports were drawing the attention of mainstream America and people took his reports as the open door to sexual freedom that had always been discreet and, in most cases, sinful behaviors. His work became the talk of the town, due mainly to the fact that sex sells; always has and always will. People began to write songs and books about Kinsey.

Martha Raye sold a half-million copies of her book <u>oh Dr. Kinsey!"</u>. Cole Porter's song TOO Darn Hot from the Tony award winning Broadway musical "Kiss Me, Kate", devoted its bridge to an analysis of the Kinsey report and the average man's sport. In 1949, Mae West, reminiscing on the days when the word sex was rarely uttered, said of Kinsey, "That guy merely makes it easy for me. Now I don't have to draw 'em any blueprints...We are both in the same business...Except I saw it first."[20]

Time magazine concluded its lead article with the following observation: Kinsey...has done for sex what Columbus did for geography', declared a pair of enthusiasts...forgetting that Columbus did not know where he was when he got there...Kinsey's work contains much that is valuable, but it must not be taken for the last word."[21]

So what was the outcome? The sexual revolution in America. Any kind of sex, anywhere, anytime. "Free love" I believe we Americans called it. Sexual freedom. If it feels good, do it. Our attitude became, "We don't need no stinking church to tell us what we can and can't do. We don't need a Bible that is outdated to guide us or condemn us. We can live any way we see fit. I surely don't need a bunch of right-wing Christians telling me how to live my life when they can't handle their own".

That has become America's attitude, and that is how we now live. All kinds of sex. All kinds of different people. If you don't like men, try women; if you like them both, call it bisexual. Sleep around. Try as many partners as you can. Which gender do you prefer? If you are not married, maybe you should live together first to see if you are sexually compatible. If you get tired of one partner, try another one. If someone hotter comes along, go for it. If you get pregnant because you were too caught up in the moment, no biggie; it's your body, just have an abortion and kill it. Who cares? It's your life, right? Do whatever works for you. Watch out for number one. You have to take care of you.

This has become the sentiment of our nation, giving people options. Do you want manual or electric windows? Would you like a chicken sandwich or a burger? Would you like that sweater in blue, green, or red? Take your pick. I know I'm being facetious, but I'm trying to show you how far we have come from what used to be One Nation Under God. And by the way, if you simply take God out of that statement, you are left with one nation under.

So, in reality, the 1960's were a reaction to the 40's and 50's as a snowball effect began to push this country further and further away from God. Now this generation is paying the heavy price of our so-called freedoms from yester-year. Not a good thing.

But there is more I want to show you!!!

CHAPTER
6

WHAT DOES THE BIBLE TEACH ABOUT HOMOSEXUALITY?

Before you read this chapter, try to stay open minded to what you are about to read. When you come across scriptures, read the scriptures slowly as it may help you understand them better. If nothing else, when you are done, at least you will know what the Bible has to say. Remember, knowledge is not too heavy a load to carry!

As a Christian and a Senior Pastor, I am supposed to know what the Bible says about almost everything in life. The Bible is literally God's blueprint of what he wants and expects from His creation, especially mankind. The Bible says we have been created in His own image (Genesis 1:27). In the Garden of Eden, when Adam and Eve sinned by disobeying a direct command from God himself, a curse came on the entire planet immediately. The second law of thermodynamics was immediately set in motion. Everything began to deteriorate and waste away. Thorns and thistles began to grow and weeds came up and began to choke out the healthy living plants. Sickness and disease became a part of planet earth. Soon storms, earthquakes, drought, and tornadoes became common place on what was once a very beautiful and pristine planet.

By the sixth chapter of Genesis, mankind itself had become so corrupt that the Bible says, God was grieved (had pain in his heart) that He had even made man on the earth(Genesis 6:6). Can you imagine the pain He must have felt? God so loved His creation, especially people; yet, everyone on the planet had turned away from God, telling Him, we don't want to follow you or your ways. The Bible says "Every inclination of every man's heart was only evil all the time" (vs. 5)

Put yourself in God's shoes. How would you feel? Only one man, Noah, was righteous (living right) in the sight of God. Because of this, God decided to start the human race all over. God appreciated Noah's willingness to still follow Him when the rest of society chose not to, so God said I will spare your family and start over with you.

He told Noah to build an Ark because He was going to destroy mankind whom He had created by sending rain on the earth to flood it (which, by the way, is quite a story beginning in Genesis chapter 6, and I don't think you would be bored reading it. The Bible is a pretty good book to read; remember, it is still the number one selling book of all time)! So, about 100 years later, that's exactly what God did. Do you realize that for those 100 years, Noah told the people what was going to happen and no one listened? It seemed like an idle tale to them. I mean, it had never rained before. The earth was watered by a vapor system coming up from the ground, so when Noah said it was going to rain, even he didn't know exactly what that meant. He was simply obeying God.

People went right on living any way they wanted with no concern whatsoever whether they were offending their Creator or not. Funny, Jesus said, "as it was in the days of Noah, so shall it be in the days when the Son of Man (Jesus himself) returns (Luke 17:26). What Jesus meant was, just like no one paid attention when Noah was preaching, and people went on living sinful lives, preachers will be preaching against sin and about God's impending judgment before Jesus returns, but people will simply go on sinning anyway.

So, the flood finally came and the earth was destroyed, along with every living thing. God had been patient, he had warned them through the preacher, he gave them time, but they just wouldn't listen. Mankind started over with just eight people: Noah, his wife, their three sons, and their wives. From them came all the people groups on the planet today. We all came from one of these three boys: Shem, Ham, or Japheth. Shem is the father of the middle eastern people, Ham is the father of the African/Ethiopian people, and Japheth is the father of the European people.

After the flood, as the people began once again to populate the earth, they started to build a city in Shinar (Babylon, or modern day

Iraq). The leader of the world at that time was a man named Nimrod. His name literally means 'Let us rebel'. Isn't that interesting? God had told Noah, just like he told Adam, to multiply and replenish the earth, and spread out. Nimrod, however, gathered everyone in one city and began to build a ziggeraut (tower) to make a name for himself. Ziggerauts which have been found around the world have on top of them the signs of the Zodiac.

Nimrod began the worship of the starry hosts of heaven (astrology; the stars and the planets), trying to create a one world religion which was anti-God. Rather than serve the Creator, all the people began to worship created things (I will break this down for you further in a moment; the scripture is found in Romans 1:18-32). At that time, after God had destroyed everyone on the planet, again, no one on earth wanted to serve the true God. Everyone just turned away.

WHAT DOES THAT HAVE TO DO WITH HOMOSEXUALITY? STAY WITH ME

As Nimrod was building this tower with the help of all the people, the world had only one language. So, in Genesis 11:7, God said I will confound their language and make them spread out over the earth so they can't work as a team The Bible literally says that, "if as one people speaking the same language they have begun to do this, then nothing they plan to do will be impossible for them" (Genesis 11:6). God caused every one of them to begin speaking a different language so no two people could understand one another (except maybe in a family cluster). This is why it was called the Tower of Babel; everyone started babbling in different languages.

Then, each family spread into different parts of the world and each of them eventually became a nation. The nations, or ethnicity's (ethnos in Greek), are called gentiles or the Nations in the Bible. What was God to do now? He had already destroyed the earth once, just a few hundred years earlier. God had a dilemma on His hands. Everyone had turned away from Him once, and now through the leadership of Nimrod, all mankind had done it again. God was going to have to come up with a new plan for humanity. But what would it be? What is the definition of insanity? To continue doing the same thing over and over, expecting different results.

God came up with another plan: Take one man and turn him into a nation. He would call this nation His people and teach them His ways. Then He would use them (this new nation) to tell all the other nations about His love and His ways. Surely this plan would work, wouldn't it? God may have thought, "If I take this one man and turn him into a nation, and through that nation I tell all the other nations what I want, then maybe they will love me and desire a relationship with me." Well, sorry God, they just don't want you!

God chose one man and decided to make him into a nation. This one man's name was Abram. God called Abram to leave his country and go to a new land. He took his wife Sarai who, by the way, was barren (couldn't have any children) and God told Abram in Genesis

12: 1-6, "I will make you into a great nation. Talk about needing faith. Go to a land where you have never been? Become a nation with a wife who can't conceive? Come on God - that takes a whole lot of faith! But God isn't a man. He is God! He only makes promises He will keep.

God changed Sarai's name, which means princess, to Sarah, meaning mother of nations (remember, she was a barren woman at this time). She heard God promise her husband Abram, whose name meant exalted father, that she, Sarah, would have a child. Sarah started laughing, saying, "shall I now have this pleasure as an old woman?" (Genesis 18:10-12). God also changed Abram's name to Abraham, meaning father of many. God heard her laugh and told them to name the boy Isaac, which means laughter. It was through Isaac that the nation of Israel would be born. This is the nation God would use to tell all the other nations about His ways and His love for them. I am getting to a point...

All the other nations, which spread out at the Tower of Babel, began to occupy lands all over the world. Each and every one of them, completely, 100%, turned away from the true, living, and creator God, and started making their own gods made out of gold, silver, wood and clay. Idols which can't talk, see, or hear, and aren't even real, but are simply man made. Remember, God, the Creator, the true God, is Holy! What does that mean? It means there is no sin, error, wrongdoing, or unfairness in him.

HERE IS MY POINT:

When all these nations started creating their own gods, these man-made gods were not, and are not, holy. So the people starting living any way they desired and doing things which God never intended for people to do. Drunkenness, orgies, drugs, murder, and evil of every kind. Prostitution with male and female prostitutes. Multiple wives and partners. Divorce and remarriage at will. Slavery, incest, murder, and corruption. These were the people groups who became nations without God. Remember what God said about the people before the flood - that every man's heart was only evil all the time? Well, they were doing it again!

When God called Abraham and Sarah to go to a new land and start a new nation, it was so they could be God's vessels of bringing back all the nations to Himself. Later on, when Abraham and Sara's family had grown to a couple of million people, God sent them to the promised land. But instead of God's nation turning all the other nations back to God, all the other nations turned God's people away from God. (Bummer! This is not what God had in mind!)

One of the many sins of the nations, and believe me, there were many, was sexual sin. I mean, let's be honest, we humans don't handle our sexuality so well. Internet pornography, x-rated movies, videos, clubs for gentlemen, strip clubs, prostitution, call girls, magazines for men and women, gay bars, child molestation, incest, promiscuity, masturbation, child sex trafficking; do I need to go on? By the way, who keeps call girls and prostitutes in business? Who is watching porn? Who are the clients of child sex rings? People. People all around us.

All the nations of the world were involved in sexual sins. It became commonplace. In fact, it was no longer looked at as sin, but rather as cultural norms. But it became even worse than that. There were no boundaries on who you had sex with. The nations thought it was OK to sleep with a niece or nephew, aunt or uncle, daughter or son in law! It got worse than that...they started having sex with animals; sheep, goats, and, well, you name it.

So now that you see where sexual sins originated from, how it was a complete rebellion against the true God of creation, it may help you to better understand why the Bible says what it says about all types of immorality.

So here are a few questions concerning sexual sins:

1)What do you say should be acceptable and not acceptable concerning human sexual behavior in society? I mean, should there be any rules at all? For example, should rape be allowed in society? How about sex with a minor? What about with a family member? Should a dad be allowed to have sex with his minor age daughter? What about a teacher at school and a student? Why are there rules at work places concerning fraternizing between coworkers? Are you getting my point? Somebody has to set some boundaries or there would be a sexual free-for-all in this country. Oh wait, there already is. LOL. My bad....

2) So who should have the final say about what is acceptable concerning right and wrong in society? Just asking!

3) On what authority would they be stating these rules? Trial and error? An internal sense of right and wrong? Another society's rules? The Bible? By what authority can someone lay down social laws that everyone needs to abide by?

4) You do admit there has to be some boundaries, right?

5) If there is a God, and He is the creator of the universe and He did create man, then maybe He does have something to say. Of course, people hate rules; always have always will. But rules are there to protect society not hurt us. So that is why God gave us social laws and also His Holy laws to live by. It was God who stated what he would or would not allow concerning how people should behave on planet earth. Listen to what the Bible says:

In the third book of the Bible, Leviticus, chapters 18 and 20, you will see what I'm talking about.
Let me outline the Book of Leviticus Chapter 18:6-27:

6 No one is to approach any close relative to have sexual relations. I am the LORD.

7 Do not dishonor your father by having sexual relations with your mother. She is your mother; do not have relations with her.

8 Do not have sexual relations with your father's wife; that would dishonor your father.

9 Do not have sexual relations with your sister, either your father's daughter or your mother's daughter, whether she was born in the same home or elsewhere.

10 Do not have sexual relations with your son's daughter or your daughter's daughter; that would dishonor you.

11 Do not have sexual relations with the daughter of your father's wife, born to your father; she is your sister.

12 Do not have sexual relations with your father's sister; she is your father's close relative.

13 Do not have sexual relations with your mother's sister, because she is your mother's close relative.

14 Do not dishonor your father's brother by approaching his wife to have sexual relations; she is your aunt.

15 Do not have sexual relations with your daughter-in-law. She is your son's wife; do not have relations with her.

16 Do not have sexual relations with your brother's wife; that would dishonor your brother.

17 Do not have sexual relations with both a woman and her daughter. Do not have sexual relations with either her son's daughter or her daughter's daughter; they are her close relatives. That is wickedness.

18 Do not take your wife's sister as a rival wife and have sexual relations with her while your wife is living.

19 Do not approach a woman to have sexual relations during the uncleanness of her monthly period.

20 Do not have sexual relations with your neighbor's wife and defile yourself with her.

21 Do not give any of your children to be sacrificed to Molech, for you must not profane the name of your God. I am the LORD.

22 Do not lie with a man as one lies with a woman; that is detestable.

23 Do not have sexual relations with an animal and defile yourself with it. A woman must not present herself to an animal to have sexual relations with it; that is a perversion.

24 Do not defile yourselves in any of these ways, because this is how the nations that I am going to drive out before you became defiled.

25 Even the land was defiled; so I punished it for its sin, and the land vomited out its inhabitants.

26 But you must keep my decrees and my laws. The native-born and the aliens living among you must not do any of these detestable things,

27 for all these things were done by the people who lived in the land before you, and the land became defiled.

I don't care who you are, you know this is **NOT** what a Holy God had in mind when He invented sex!

That's right. God invented sex. Can you believe it? If He created it, and He is Holy, then sex must be a good thing, right? YES! But look at what else the nations were doing:

Leviticus 20:9-21 goes on to say:

9 If anyone curses his father or mother, he must be put to death. He has cursed his father or his mother, and his blood will be on his own head.

10 If a man commits adultery with another man's wife--with the wife of his neighbor--both the adulterer and the adulteress must be put to death.

11 If a man sleeps with his father's wife, he has dishonored his father. Both the man and the woman must be put to death; their blood will be on their own heads.

12 If a man sleeps with his daughter-in-law, both of them must be put to death. What they have done is a perversion; their blood will be on their own heads.

13 If a man lies with a man as one lies with a woman, both of them have done what is detestable. They must be put to death; their blood will be on their own heads.

14 If a man marries both a woman and her mother, it is wicked. Both he and they must be burned in the fire, so that no wickedness will be among you.

15 If a man has sexual relations with an animal, he must be put to death, and you must kill the animal.

16 If a woman approaches an animal to have sexual relations with it, kill both the woman and the animal. They must be put to death; their blood will be on their own heads.

17 If a man marries his sister, the daughter of either his father or his mother, and they have sexual relations, it is a disgrace. They must be cut off before the eyes of their people. He has dishonored his sister and will be held responsible.

18 If a man lies with a woman during her monthly period and has sexual relations with her, he has exposed the source of her flow, and she has also uncovered it. Both of them must be cut off from their people.

19 Do not have sexual relations with the sister of either your mother or your father, for that would dishonor a close relative; both of you would be held responsible.

20 If a man sleeps with his aunt, he has dishonored his uncle. They will be held responsible; they will die childless.

21 If a man marries his brother's wife, it is an act of impurity; he has dishonored his brother. They will be childless.

22 Keep all my decrees and laws and follow them, so that the land where I am bringing you to live may not vomit you out.

The Bible speaks loud and clear concerning sexual sin. Listen to what Paul the Apostle says: **"But among you (Christians), there must not be even a hint of sexual immorality or impurity** (Ephesians 5:3). Not even a hint! Another translation says, "do not let it be named even once among you". That is unequivocal to say the least! Plain and simple!

So what is sexual sin? (This is where I can't pull any punches). **I am speaking to the Christian and the non-Christian, to the gay person and the straight: Any sex, outside of marriage, in the eyes of God is sin!**

I didn't say in the eyes of man, I said in the eyes of God. In the eyes of man, everyone has an opinion, pick the one you like. If you like the person whose opinion is "anything goes" than have at it. If you like the opinion of the person who says all that matters is that you care about the other person well, there you go. By the way, what is your opinion

If you want to know what God says and demands, you have to read His word, the Bible. You see, in the beginning, God intended for people to have families and populate the earth. This was His design. And in case you have forgotten, this is still His universe, and always will be, until He rolls the whole thing up like a garment and makes a new one. His perfect plan was for a man and a woman to be committed in a life long relationship which He called marriage. Through the union of a man and woman (husband / wife relationship), they were to have children. The parents were to teach their children about God and His ways.

Instead, when the nations spread out at the Tower of Babel, they stopped thanking Him and worshiping Him as God, and their children ended up knowing nothing about the holiness and righteousness of God. For example, did your parents tell you about the holiness and righteousness of God? Did you grow up learning about a kind, compassionate, and loving God, as well as a Holy and equitable God? If not, you are living your life the way you choose to live it, and your belief system about right and wrong is based on a combination of the opinions of many other people.

You probably want to argue with me right now. But the fact is, you probably only hang out with and tolerate people who see most things the way you do. If someone doesn't hold to your opinion of how life should be lived, you simply spend little to no time with them. Others who don't agree with your stance on things aren't as bright as you are and are too narrow minded for you. This includes Christians and non-Christians. We are all that way.

WHEN SEX LOST ITS ORIGINAL INTENT

This is the scripture I was referring to earlier when I said that after the people spread out from the Tower of Babel under Nimrod's rule, they started worshiping created things rather then the creator. They stopped thanking and worshiping God as God, so their thinking became futile.

So when did sex lose its original intent? When the nations at the Tower of Babel spread out to different parts of the world and turned away from the one true God, who is Holy, to serve false, man-made gods, they began to turn away from all the good things God had intended for them.

Listen to what Romans 1:18-28 says:

18 The wrath of God is being revealed from heaven against all the godlessness and wickedness of men who suppress the truth by their wickedness,

19 since what may be known about God is plain to them, because God has made it plain to them.

20 For since the creation of the world God's invisible qualities-- his eternal power and divine nature--have been clearly seen, being understood from what has been made, so that men are without excuse.

21 **For although they knew God**, they neither glorified him as God nor gave thanks to him, but their thinking became futile and their foolish hearts were darkened.

22 Although they claimed to be wise, they became fools

23 and exchanged the glory of the immortal God for images made to look like mortal man and birds and animals and reptiles.

24 Therefore God gave them over in the sinful desires of their hearts to **sexual impurity** for the degrading of their bodies with one another.

25 They exchanged the truth of God for a lie, and worshiped and served created things rather than the Creator--who is forever praised. Amen.

26 Because of this, God gave them over to shameful lusts. **Even their women exchanged natural relations for unnatural ones.**

*27 In the same way the **men also abandoned natural relations with women** and were inflamed with lust for one another. **Men committed indecent acts with other men**, and received in themselves the due penalty for their perversion.*

*28 **Furthermore, since they did not think it worthwhile to retain the knowledge of God, he gave them over to a depraved mind, to do what ought not to be done.***

Do you get it? Because mankind stopped worshiping and thanking the one true Holy God, they were open to every form of false religion and every kind of sinful practice, which of course, included sexual sins. Men went after other men. Women exchanged natural relations for unnatural ones. As it said in Leviticus 18 and 20, they did everything they could think of sexually. Why? Because they weren't following the ways of a Holy God.

Sexual sin includes every kind of sexual act outside of marriage. Plain and simple; period! What about masturbation? I'll explain that in a moment. Any two people who are not married and engage in sex, are in sin. Does that sound narrow minded? Take it up with God. He invented sex. Maybe He didn't know what He was doing. Maybe God's definition of sex should have a broader use than just in marriage. I mean, if He gave us each a sex drive, what did He expect us to do with it?

Not only is the Bible clear about sexual sin, but it speaks to different kinds of sexual sin. Again, the Bible speaks against all sins, especially sexual ones; **it tells us to flee sexual sin (1 Corinthians 6:18), and this includes, but is not limited to, homosexuality.** Sexual sin is talked about often in our church due to what I mentioned earlier, that we have so many visitors and new attendees, and the fact that I am dealing with human beings.

What do you think non-Christian or non-church people are doing about their sex drives? Probably not controlling it. Whether it's one night stands, pornography, masturbation, sleeping with their boyfriend or girlfriend, prostitutes or call girls, the internet or magazines, almost everyone is having some kind of sex. Please remember, my job as a minister is not to give my opinion, but God's Word. I know people get upset with preachers, some because they are boring, others because they use the pulpit for a personal soapbox, some because they are hypocritical, and many because they preach God's truth unashamedly. The old saying "don't get mad at the messenger" is oh so true about real Bible teachers.

The Bible is very clear on sexual sin, including homosexuality. God calls it sin. God intended for there to be one man and one woman, to have a family, raise kids, and to teach them His standards of holiness. However, because as humans we don't want anyone telling us what to do or how to live, we get mad at preachers. In addition, when Christians themselves start judging people instead of showing the love of Christ to them, it just compounds the problem.

So, to summarize and bring into focus, the nations perverted God's original intent for sex. A long time ago sexual sin became common place for humans. Now, even here in America we demand our freedoms. Freedoms to do what we want, when we want, and how we want - and we don't want anyone trying to tell us what is right or wrong, sinful or allowable. We simply want what we want and that's all there is to it. Basically the world says, "You leave me alone peacher, and I'll leave you alone."

Would somebody wake up and smell the coffee !?

CHAPTER 7

THE SEDUCTION OF MASTURBATION

Pastor, is masturbation allowed?" I am asked this question quite regularly by a host of people, most of them Christian, but not all of them. What does a person do who has been married and now they are divorced, or their spouse has died? What do people do about their sexual desires then? Is it okay to self gratify?

"Pastor, I am single. What do I do about my sexuality? Am I really supposed to do nothing about my sex drive until I get married? Come on!" This is another question I am frequently asked. This does not account for all the people who haven't asked, yet are dealing with this issue and are too afraid to ask. Everyone has to manage their own sex drive, just like they have to manage their own eating habits, drinking habits, and everything else that pertains to their individual person.

People in our church are simply human, just like you; no different, just trying to do life. Even though they may call themselves Christians, they struggle with what is right and wrong, acceptable or not acceptable, just like you and me. We are still human beings who put on one pant leg or pantyhose at a time. They want to serve God in every way, but they have silent, unspoken questions concerning their private lives which they are seeking answers for, maybe just like you. They want solid answers that make sense, and for the Christian, those answers come from the Word of God.

They want answers they can understand and apply to their lives. They aren't looking for someone's opinion. They are too smart for that. They are really asking what God says concerning issues of life that we all seem to struggle with. Again, the easiest thing to do is to just remove God from our belief system, put the Bible away or say that it can't be trusted, that it was written by men who probably manipulated the truth, and now everyone is left to their own opinion. That makes life so much easier, doesn't it? But, what if there is a real God, and the Bible is His love letter to all humanity? Does the Bible address masturbation? Yes, I believe it does.

Going back to Jesus' Sermon on the Mount in Matthew chapters 5-7, Jesus said, **"If a man looks lustfully at a woman, he has already committed adultery with her in his heart** (Matt 5:27-28). The very next sentence continues, **If your right eye causes you to sin, gouge it out and throw it away. It is better for you to lose one part of your body than for your whole body to be thrown into hell. If your right**

hand causes you to sin, cut it off and throw it away. It is better for you to lose one part of your body than for your whole body to go into hell (vs. 29-30).

LET ME EXPLAIN

The whole context of this passage is sexual sin. Lusting and adultery. Jesus said if your right eye causes you to sin, gouge it out and throw it away. Jesus is using illustrative language. For most people the right eye is the dominant or stronger eye. The statement "if it causes you to sin" means if you can't control what you look at, in this case lusting after another person (the word lusting in Greek is blepo, meaning to stare with an intense longing), then it would be better for you to gouge out your eye. Jesus is using exaggerated speech to make a point. In other words, you *better* do something about your lack of self control.

The thought continues, "If your right hand causes you to sin"... Again, what is the context? Sexual sin. He seems to be saying that when you lust after someone and then use your right hand (the dominant hand for most people) to satisfy your lust (masturbate or self gratify), you are sinning. Why?

Because the person you are self gratifying about is not your spouse. Just because you didn't actually have sex with them, you did in your mind and in your heart. Anyone you lust after (which is what masturbation is) who is not your spouse, you are using to gratify your own sexual wants, and in the eyes of God this is sin.

Let me continue with candor (by the way, these are issues almost never ever talked about in churches today). If you are married and are away from your spouse for an extended period of time, or they are physically ill, or may have even passed away, and you then pleasure yourself thinking of them, you can technically get away with that before God; I mean, they are your spouse. However, if your spouse is away from you for an extended period, maybe God wants to teach you self control, or wants you to be in a season of prayer with fasting. God's grace will sustain you so that you are not burning with lust but you will have a part to play.

Here is how: Sex is fueled by sex. What I mean is, you can't look at provocative material and then not expect to get turned on or want to do something about it. You can't put sexually stimulating stuff in front of your eyes and mind, think about sex all the time, and then not get turned on. The reason people watch or keep themselves entertained with sexual things is so they can get turned on. They are feeding a lust in themselves and the more they feed it, the more they want. As I just said, sex is fueled by sex! God wants to clean up your thought life and by doing so you will see that your sex drive gets turned down to a simmer. This is something to think about. If you were to stop feeding your mind sexual things, you would be amazed at the difference in your life.

I regularly have unmarried couples come in for counseling with me. They want to serve God and keep their relationship pure until they get married, but they come in and say they don't understand why they keep falling into sexual sin. So I ask them to tell me about what they are doing on their dates that leads them to falling sexually. They usually say they start off fine, dinner and a movie. But then they go back to her place, put on some Luther Vandros, crack a bottle of wine, start necking, and then they can't figure out why they always end up having sex. Hello? You can't put yourself in a place where you excite yourself sexually and then expect not to do something about it.

The sex act was meant to be fulfilled once it has begun. But only by two people who are married. That's why the Bible says, "Do not arouse or awaken love before it is ready" (Song of Solomon 2:7). You might ask, "Then what do I do about my sex drive"? First of all, stop inflaming it! You won't know how strong you are until you stop feeding your sexual urges with sexual stuff. Try it, and see what happens.

Let's be honest, almost always you have someone in mind every time you commit this act called masturbation. You enter into a fantasy of someone you know or someone you've seen, either in real life, or in the movies, or by looking at something pornographic. You then begin to think about them in a sexual way and as you continue to do so, you then feel the sexual urge which you believe you must now gratify. So then, you self gratify, thinking (lusting) about them. The more you give in to sex, the more you will want it. I will say it again, satisfying your sexual urges doesn't make them go away, it actually inflames them.

God understands our sexual needs. He gave them to us. But like in everything else in our lives, we are responsible to manage them. You can't keep putting those kind of provocative things in front of you and not get turned on. You can't keep sexually desiring every attractive person you see, then go home and satisfy your urges with them on your mind. God's plan was that every man would have his own wife, and every woman would have her own husband (1 Corinthians 7:3). Our sexual needs are to be met within the confines of marriage.

Realistically speaking, I also realize that people will gratify themselves sexually one way or another. If that is inevitable for you, you might want to do your best NOT having someone in mind. I'm not quite sure how exactly you do that, but...

Some of you are probably thinking right now, "Dude, are you like, serious? If I'm single or divorced, am I supposed to do nothing about my sex drive? Give me a break"! Masturbation is not the unpardonable sin. But it is a self control issue. I know for some people, sex is one of the greatest pleasures in life. I agree. So does God. He invented it. But each of us needs to have a life partner, a husband or a wife. If your spouse is sick or on a business trip or something of that nature, thinking about them, especially with their approval, I'm sure could be exciting for both of you. But to gratify about anyone else is lust, plain and simple.

Why am I even discussing this issue of masturbation? To show you that we, as humans, inflame ourselves sexually, engage in some type of sex act, and then say there is nothing wrong with that. Well, God's Word says there is, if it is outside the confines of marriage. You may not like it, may not even agree with it, but you can't deny that is what the Bible teaches. I wrote this to demonstrate that people are inflaming themselves sexually with all kinds of sexually explicit material and because of this there is now a sexual free-for-all in America which everyone seems to want except God! It is one of the things which is helping to deteriorate our great country.

CHAPTER
8

COMING OUT

W e have dozens of people in our church who at one time lived the gay life, and now, after finding Jesus Christ as their Lord and Savior, are living heterosexual or celibate lives. Some have shared their story with me. What I find most intriguing is that all those whom I have talked with have told me of the different events in their lives that started them living and practicing the gay lifestyle. The most common ones are: some sort of dysfunctional relationship with their father; sexual abuse by someone older and usually of the same sex; an abusive or very dissatisfying heterosexual relationship which caused them to look elsewhere; being in a career where others in that line of work were predominately gay; a 'curious-type' sexual encounter with the same sex which was enjoyable; having had feminine or masculine characteristics growing up and being teased and labeled as being gay.

Many of these people upon looking back on their childhood, believe that they were attracted to the same sex from a fairly young age.

These are the predominant backgrounds of the people I have talked to and what they have told me. For example, one older lady said that she got involved in a lesbian relationship for about 10 years because her husband left her for another woman. She said she was so hurt by the destruction of her family, that when another woman came to her rescue and understood her, they simply fell into a sexual relationship. The other woman was so understanding and so sensitive and caring, it just happened She has since gone back to a heterosexual life and also remarried. This was - and is - a Christian woman!

There is also the story of a woman who lived the lesbian life for years and is now a celibate Christian woman since coming to Christ. Her story was that her father was an overbearing and very hard man to please. She loved her daddy, but it seemed so difficult to make him happy. Never could she talk back without a slap, had to keep an "A"grade point average, was not allowed to date or even be around boys, and seldom was allowed to go to social functions. Her response to that when she went off to college was to go buck wild.

She began having multiple sexual encounters with both males and females, and for a time would have considered herself bisexual. However, she leaned more toward the lesbian lifestyle. After accepting Jesus as Lord, she realized why she had chosen to live that way. She told me she realized that it was her way of rebelling against her father and she then became addicted to sex, especially with women. She is now helping others break their sexual addictions with her testimony.

Another young man who is still struggling with his sexual identity said that growing up, he didn't feel as close to his father as it seemed his siblings did. That, mixed with having some feminine characteristics early on and being teased and called "gay boy" caused him to seek out male companionship. Adding to that, he was tricked into a sexual encounter by an older male who sexually abused him which caused him great confusion. The stories go on and on. Like the man who had a very harsh and difficult to please father, and as he got older starting experimenting with alcohol and drugs. As he started hanging out in that environment, he tried a gay encounter, enjoyed it, and never turned back until many years had gone by.

Maybe your story is similar, or not. You may have your own set of circumstances. Only you and God really know all the details. Maybe being lesbian or gay has become your very identity and lifestyle of choice. You know how to live and act in those arenas. You have now become so convinced that this is just who you are, you see no reason or need to change and you really don't want to hear what the Good Book has to say.

I also know there are many people living the gay life right now who think that God is perfectly accepting of it and that He is a loving, caring, and forgiving God, who is OK with them as long as they are in a loving, committed, monogamous relationship. They have been told, or somehow believe themselves that God, because He is so loving, would never judge them because they are good people, upstanding citizens, hard working, honest, and committed to one person, even if they are of the same sex.

As I stated in the preface of this book, there is a BIG difference between God loving all of us, and Him being pleased with all of us. He loves us. He proved that by sending His son to die on the cross. But is He pleased with all our choices? No, He is not. Remember, He is a Holy God. Like parents who love their children and yet have to chastise them when they disobey or act disrespectfully, God is the same with us. If we continue to do things we know are not according to His will and purpose, there will be a price to pay. **So let me state again**: There is a BIG difference between God loving us and Him being pleased with us.

ARE YOU WILLING TO TRY?

As I talk with those who want to serve Christ, yet, feel they are trapped by their sexual orientation, I want them to know what God is asking of them; God does not ask us to do things we can't do without His help and strength. He understands that for most people it will be a process over time whereby He walks them through to a new way of life. (He is not saying you must stop your homosexual desires immediately and go straight. At least most people will not have that experience, although it is possible and some do). He is saying, "I want you to leave the homosexual lifestyle and reverse your course (repent) and I will make you brand new from the inside out". This is where His grace and mercy is extended along with great patience. This is how God really is. Now wait, before you get mad.

If you are not willing to really try something, I mean really try, how will you know if you can or can't do it? For example, I can not do a back flip. In fact, I am not willing to even try! But if I am not willing to even try, then I am right I can't do a back flip. However, to be totally accurate, I should really say, I am not willing to **SEE** if I can do a back flip.

But, if I were willing to try a back flip, with the help of a competent coach, I truly might be able to do one. I will never know if I don't try. I can't really say I am unable to do one unless I am willing to try. What I am saying is, if you gave yourself a real chance at dating the opposite sex with a romantic intent, God will help you all the way. (Some of you might say that you did try the straight life and it didn't work for you, or maybe you simply like the gay life better. Someone might say, "I'm gay and the opposite sex doesn't attract me." I want to challenge your thinking on all these).

If God gave you the gift of being single then you could call yourself asexual or celibate. Very few people, however, have this gift. If you deeply desire a companion in your life, which would be a good indication that you may not have the gift of being single, then I promise you God will teach you how to change your orientation. It will not happen overnight, at least in most cases. That is why I said you must give yourself a real chance, with your whole heart.

I understand you are comfortable living on your lily pad. But there is a whole new Island a few feet away! I know it is uncomfortable, unfamiliar, foreign, and different. But you won't know if you like this Island until you get away from what is familiar and comfortable and try something new. The Island belongs to God, and it is filled with love and strength and power. You will be amazed at how much you can accomplish with God on your side. Romans 8:31 says, "if God be for us, who can be against us." Jump little frog, jump!

A REAL LIFE STORY THAT WILL BLOW YOUR MIND !

Let me tell you of one woman in our church who was completely immersed in the gay life and is now living a heterosexual and fulfilled life, as she states it (and there are many, many others), to show that with God's help, if a person is willing to make the changes, they can. She is just one of the multitude of people who have said 'yes' to God's will and His ways, and have found total happiness; but, it wasn't easy.

We have a group of women who come to our church who have recently been incarcerated. Many of them come out of prison with addictions to drugs and alcohol and are steeped in the gay life. Their stories are varied and sad. They come to our church through this program and they find acceptance and love from our congregation. In addition, they begin (many for the first time) to hear the teaching of the Word of God and they learn principles of how to make positive life changes which they are able to do through the power of Jesus Christ.

It is absolutely amazing to watch this transformation take place in their lives.

This one woman in particular, we will call her Sam, came to our church looking very masculine. She had a man's haircut, weighed about 210 pounds, wore black jeans and army type boots with a chain hanging from her pocket and a host of tattoos. It was obvious she was the dominant one in her gay relationship. She wore men's cologne and no make-up; she just looked tough.

After sitting in our church for some time and hearing the teachings from the Bible concerning sexual sin, she said it began to bother her whenever she was intimate with her girlfriend, or any woman for that matter. She began to feel dirty, and she knew that what she was doing was not pleasing to God. So she silently began to pray for God to help her make some changes. She was scared to death to make the changes because this was all she knew. She really didn't know if she could fully surrender to what God was showing her, but she was willing to try.

That is one of the greatest hindrances I have found as I talk to people trying to come out of the gay life; they either really don't believe they can, or, in their heart, they really aren't ready to make a 100% effort. I never said it would be easy, in fact, just the opposite is true. We are talking a lifestyle change, becoming a whole new you and being willing to turn and walk in a different direction with a whole new identity. Not an easy thing to do for anybody - but it is not impossible!

So, as Sam continued to pray and ask God for help, she realized there were some things she would need to do in order to live this new life. She began to let her hair grow. Then she stopped buying cologne and bought perfume instead. She also began wearing make-up, just a little at first until she got comfortable, and a little more as time went on. She also changed the style of her clothes, all the while fighting through the fears of what others might think. I mean, this had been her identity the majority of her life. What would her peers say? But she kept praying and pressing forward.

However, the next big step was coming. Would she be able to make the switch from lesbian desires to opposite sex attraction and relationship? This scared her and concerned her more than any of the other fears. How would she know? What would be the test? What if she just couldn't do it? But, she stood her ground and continued praying and trusting God. His Word assures the believer that, we can do all things through Christ who strengthens us (Philippians 4:13), and, "Greater is He that is in me, than he that is in the world" (1John 4:4). But would it work for me, she thought?

This next part I do not recommend, but this is what Sam shared with me of her experience coming out.

Sam had a childhood friend, a male, who had always told her one day he would marry her. She would just wrote him off as a trash talker, and never paid him much mind. However, it stuck in the back of her head that he had constantly said this to her, but didn't he realize that she liked women? What would make him think she would ever be with him, or even want to? Silly daydreaming boy, she thought. But remember, never say never.

Well, as she was making all these external changes, she began to look in the mirror and see a different person. She began to see in the reflection of that mirror, a pretty girl, attractive figure, nice smile, and a friendly demeanor. Something she wasn't used to seeing before. What was happening was that God was changing her heart, and from that heart change it began to change everything else about her. She couldn't believe it herself. "Is this really me, a new me", she thought?

Then, it happened: a man she had never met before found her very attractive. Her biggest fears were now being placed right before her. What would she do? What would she be able to do? What if she just felt no connection or attraction? But she simply had to find out. (This is the part I don't recommend. I'll explain why in a moment).

They went on a couple of dates, and then he made his move. He wanted to take her to bed. All the while she too needed to know if she could do this - lie down with a man. It had always been women she had been with. She knew how to operate in that arena, with the same sex. She was the dominant one. She gave the orders, made the moves, said who would do what and when. But now she was in the role of female, with a real life male wanting to have his way. Would she? Could she? But, she just had to know. So she went for it.

As I said earlier, when you are making a godly life change, you have to fully give yourself over to doing what God is asking. Then, and only then can you look back and say that you have truly tried. You can fake trying, make a halfhearted attempt, but you will always wonder if you could have really done it or not. By "it" I mean, going

180 degrees in the opposite direction from the same sex to the opposite sex. This is what Sam did. She gave it a real try; from make-up to perfume, to a complete a wardrobe change, to dating a male. And guess what? Today she is happily married with kids and says she has absolutely no desire for the same sex! None.

This can be you too. Remember, she never believed it would happen to her either.

Now, also remember that I said I wouldn't recommend you do what she did. Let me explain:

Humanly speaking, I can understand her wondering if she could make the total switch sexually from gay to straight. I can also understand her thinking that she had to experiment sexually with the opposite sex to see if she were really able to do this or not. However, she could have done this by faith in God also. Let me further explain that the changes she made were from the heart; she had become a new person in Christ Jesus. God doesn't do a partial work in us, He does a complete work. God will give you the strength in every way to completely fulfill his perfect will.

She didn't need to experiment to see if she could make the switch all the way over; God would have completed the work in her by her faith in God. When she told herself that she didn't know if she could make the switch from gay to straight, she was doubting the powerful work of the Holy Spirit in her life. This is what caused her to believe that she had to experiment first. However, the problem now becomes one of sin - sexual sin with the opposite sex. I told you earlier that any sex outside of marriage is sin in the eyes of God. So, when she lay down with this man sexually, she was committing fornication, or sex outside of marriage. The Holy Spirit of God will never lead us to sin, even if it seems reasonable!

If you are coming out of the gay life, just like everybody else, you will have to trust God to bring you all the way through. But you have to be honest with yourself; do you really want to give yourself a fair chance? Are you really willing to turn and follow God? Will you really let other people help you? These are questions you have to ask yourself first. If your answer is yes to all of these, I promise you, God will enable you to make a complete change, just like Sam did.

As I stated at the beginning of this book, I am just a messenger. My job in life is to live and preach the Word of God, the Bible. I am not perfect, and quite honestly, I sin everyday, one way or another. Again, sin being defined as not living up to God's standard of what is right or wrong, not man's. If I were only being judged by man's standard of whether I am a good person or not, then in the eyes of many people, I would be considered a pretty good person, just like you. But I too am judged, not by man alone, but by God's Word - and according to His standard, I fall way short!

The people who believe the Bible to be the Word of God and the final authority, who were once involved in the gay life and have since come out, understand the way they were living was not God's original intent for mankind. Once you accept Jesus as your Lord, you must acknowledge that you are a sinner. After you come to this realization, you must repent. This means to turn from your sin and go in another direction. I am not saying this will be easy. For many, like Sam, to come out of the gay lifestyle is very difficult, but it IS possible.

There are many churches and ministries which can help you and will commit themselves to you walking in your new identity. The power of Jesus Christ is greater than any force in heaven and earth. Listen to what the Bible says in Ephesians 1:19-21, *"That power is like the working of his mighty strength which he exerted in Christ when he raised him from the dead and seated him at his right hand in the heavenly places, far above all rule and authority, power and dominion, and every title that can be given, not only in the present age but also in the one to come"*.

What does that mean exactly? That Jesus, and the power of His name, is the greatest power in the universe and always will be. It is above every name or title that humans can give. Things like disease, bondage, sin, abuse, addiction, lifestyle, thoughts, attitudes, sickness, loneliness, depression, you name it and the name of Jesus is greater and more powerful. Listen to this, "I can do all things through Christ who strengthens me"(Philippians 4:13).

No matter what you have been through, where you have been, or what you have done, the blood of Jesus Christ will wash it all away and give you a brand new start in life. That is why it is called being Born Again. He gives you a brand new start. He will allow His Spirit, the Holy Spirit, to come and live inside you. That means God Himself will come and dwell within you. You will have a new nature, God's nature.

The Bible says that when people give their heart and life to Jesus Christ, God adopts them into His family. You become a child of God by faith in Jesus Christ (Galatians 3:26). Many people erroneously believe that every human being is a child of God. In one sense they are, in that they were created in His image. But in another sense, they are not. Jesus said in John 8:44, "You are of your father the devil". Wow!

There is an ancient city in Greece called Corinth. I have been there and I have seen the ruins. Interestingly enough, they uncovered a V.D. Clinic which was in existence over 2,000 years ago! This city was known for its sexual laxity and immoral behavior. In fact, to have it said that, "You act like a Corinthian" meant you were very loose in your morals and practiced vices of every kind, including orgies, drunkenness, homosexuality, male prostitution, slander, and whatever else you could think of. People in San Francisco would blush at some of the behaviors going on in Corinth. Well, maybe.

Paul the Apostle was literally sent there by the Spirit of God to preach the gospel of Jesus Christ. Now remember, these were ungodly and immoral people, even by their own standards. So, Paul goes to Corinth and proclaims Jesus Christ as Lord and Savior and many people turned from their sin lifestyles and began to follow Christ. However, like for many people coming out of the gay lifestyle today, including Sam, it is a process, just like it was for the Corinthian people.

Paul stayed in Corinth for 18 months and taught them victorious Christian living and then had to leave to go to other cities to preach the gospel. After being gone for some time, he began hearing reports that the people were falling back into all kinds of old habits and lifestyles. So, Paul writes the letter known as 1 Corinthians. Listen to what he says in 1 Corinthians 6:9-11: *"Do you not know that the wicked will not inherit the kingdom of God? Do not be deceived: Neither the sexually immoral nor idolaters nor adulterers nor male prostitutes nor homosexual offenders nor thieves nor the greedy nor drunkards nor slanderers nor swindlers will inherit the kingdom of God. And that is what some of you were. But you were washed, you were sanctified, you were justified in the name of the Lord Jesus Christ and by the Spirit of our God"*.

Please understand, Jesus came to save sinners. Everyone in Corinth was a sinner. Everyone who ever got saved in Corinth was a sinner. The whole church there was filled with ex-sinners just like you and me. Some struggled more than others trying to give up life-long habits and addictions. But please remember, God is compassionate and gracious, slow to anger, abounding in love (Psalm 103:8).

For everyone of us, living the Christian life is a process. It is a life of growing and learning to be more and more like Jesus. Some may do it quicker than others, but the good news is that God doesn't give up on us. We may give up on Him, but He will never give up on us. As Philippians 1:6 says, "he who began a good work in you will carry it on to completion." The fact is, we all stumble in many ways, but if you are serious about making godly changes in your life, God will, by the power of His Holy Spirit working in you and with you will enable you to not only make the changes but also continue the process of being victorious in those changes for the rest of your life.

It is only by accepting Jesus Christ as your Lord and Savior that you become a child of God, adopted into the family of God by God Himself. The difference between when a person adopts a child and when God adopts a child, is that God gives them His very nature! They become just like their father (Heavenly Father, that is). A human parent can't give you their nature when they adopt you. They can nurture you, provide for you, protect, instruct and even train you in the things of life, but they are incapable of giving you their nature. That is what it means to be born from above or born again

(John 3:3). You recieve God's very own Spirit living in you.

Whenever anyone, gay or straight, gives their life to Christ, they are now given a new nature which overrides, conquers, and puts to death their old nature which has sin as its master. Now your new master is God himself who is living in you. Now I am no longer bound to the old habits and patterns which used to control and dominate my life. Why? Because if the Son sets you free, you will be free indeed (John 8:36)!

When God lives in you, 1 John 4:4 says: "You, dear children, are from God and have overcome them, because the one **WHO IS IN YOU** is greater than the one who is in the world". You can be set free from any sin, bondage, addiction, lifestyle, mindset, habit, and controlling substance or behavior. It may be a process out for many people, and some will experience victory and freedom quicker than others, but you can do it with God on your side and with you on His.

In most cases it is not easy; but then again, what in life which is valuable or worthwhile is easy? Scores of people have come out, all the way out, and they are living productive and fruitful new lives in Christ Jesus. And you can too!

First, you must begin by acknowledging that you are a sinner, and your sins are many. Next, you must choose to repent (turn away from) and renounce them as a part of your life. Then, you must believe with all your heart that Jesus Christ has been raised from the dead by the power of God. Next, you must say (confess) with your mouth, that Jesus is Lord, your Lord, and Lord of all. The Bible says that when a person believes with their heart that God raised Jesus from the dead, and confesses with their mouth that Jesus is Lord, they are saved! (Romans 10:9-10).

Now, you must find someone who is mature in the Christian faith to keep you accountable. Remember, accountability is given, not taken. What I mean is, you have to be honest with someone and allow them to keep you accountable for your thoughts and behaviors. If you lie to them and only tell them selective things, they can't really keep you accountable because you are not letting them. It requires complete honesty.

For some, coming out of the gay lifestyle will be the hardest thing you will have ever done, but you can do it! You can. Yes, you can.

It doesn't mean you won't have any more thoughts which are wrong or sinful; on the contrary. You will still have many tempting thoughts and desires, just like heterosexuals do. Only now, you will learn how to combat them and overcome them. If you expect never to be tempted by them again, you are only kidding yourself and the devil is lying to you. He will say things in your mind like "If you were really a Christian, you wouldn't still have these thoughts. Look at you, trying to pretend you are something when you are not. You know you want to go back to the gay life, don't you?"

But, you will learn to fight the devil by the Word of God. The Word of God, the Bible, is what Jesus used against the devil when for 40 days he tempted Jesus to turn against his father. When He, Jesus, kept quoting the Word of God to the devil, the devil left Him alone. In fact, Jesus' brother, James, wrote in his letter in the Bible, "Submit yourselves, then, to God. Resist the devil, and he will flee from you" (James 4:7). Is that a cool promise from God or what?

Peter, the disciple who walked with Jesus, also said, "Be self controlled and alert. Your enemy the devil prowls around like a roaring lion looking for someone to devour. Resist him, standing firm in the faith, because you know that your brothers throughout the world are undergoing the same kind of suffering" (1 Peter 5:8-9).

So the key to victorious Christian living for anybody is, submitting to the Holy Spirit (God) who lives inside us and leads us (Romans 8:14), resisting the devil by speaking the Word of God to every situation you face and then, not giving in to the temptations or believing the lies Satan throws at us. Is that clear? If you give in to them, or believe them, convincing yourself of his lies, you will end up right back where you started. This is why many go right back to their sin even though they really believe in Jesus.

Remember, it is not simply believing in Jesus that makes someone a Christian; even the devil believes Jesus is the son of God, and I guarantee you Satan is not saved. It is belief in Jesus Christ whereby we live a life of obedience, not perfection, but obedience, that identifies us as a Christian. We all stumble and make mistakes in many ways, even Jesus' brother James said so (James 3:2). But, Jesus said, if you love me, you will obey my commands" (John 14:15). You do not continue to live a life of habitual sin. You become dead to sin, and then you have to keep putting your sinful desires to death by the things I listed above: submitting to God, resisting the devil, speaking truth and quoting scripture, not listening to lies and becoming an obedient Christian.

It is my sincere desire, hope, and prayer, that you will choose Jesus Christ as your Lord and Savior, and that you will allow him to set you free. I pray that the lies of Satan will be unmasked and uncovered, and maybe for the first time in your life, you will truly be set free.

God bless you,

Pastor Gary

NOTES

1. BBC Mobile News (2008, June 16). *Scans see 'gay brain differences'*. Retrieved January 20, 2011, from http://news.bbc.co.uk/2/hi/health/7456588.stm.

2..BBC Mobile News (2008, June 16).

3. BBC Mobile News (2008, June 16).

4 . Whitehead, N.E. (n.d.). *The importance of twin studies*. Retrieved July 27, 2010, from http://www.narth.com/docs/whitehead2.html

5. Whitehead, N.E. (n.d.).

6. Whitehead, N.E. (n.d.).

7. Whitehead, N.E. (n.d.).

8. Greenberg, J. S., Bruess, C. E. Conklin, S. C. (2011, 4th ed). *Sexual Orientation. Exploring the dimensions of human sexuality* (pp.360-361). Jones and Bartlett Publishers: Sudbury, MA

9. Greenberg, J. S., Bruess, C. E. Conklin, S. C. (2011, 4th ed).

10. Toufexis, Anastasia. (1995, November 13). *New Evidence of a ?ay Gene Time Magazine*, Vol 146, Issue 20, p.95

11. Whitehead, N.E. (n.d.).

12. Boice, J. M. (1979). *Sin against man, sin against God. Genesis: an expositional commentary*. Zondervan Publishing House: Grand Rapids, MI

13. Boice, J. M. (1979).

14. Boice, J. M. (1979).

15. Boice, J. M. (1979).

16. Alfred Kinsey: Clyde Eugene (1998 reprint of 1948 original) *Sexual Behavior in the Human Male* Indiana Universit Press p.p. 178-180

17. Same as above

18. Reumann, Miriam 2005 American Sexual Character: Sex, Gender, and National Identity in Kinsey Reports. Archives of sexual behavior (University of California Press, Berkeley: Springer Netherlands Volume 36 #5: 294

19. *"How to Stop Gin Rummy"* Time. 1948-03-01

20. Rich, Frank (2004 12-12) The Plot against Sex in America New York Times

21. Time. 1953-08-24 (Women)

BIBLICAL QUOTATIONS

All scripture quoted are in NIV, unless otherwise noted

Genesis 1:27	Luke 19:10
Genesis 1:28	John 3:3
Genesis 6:6	John 6:37
Genesis 9:5-6	John 8:1-11
Genesis 11:6	John 8:5
Genesis 18:10-12	John 8:36
Genesis 25:24-26	John 8:44
Exodus 20:13	John 14:15
Exodus 20:16	John 12:1-11
Leviticus 18:6-27	Romans 1:18-28
Leviticus 20:9-21	Romans 3:10
Song of Solomon 2:7	Romans 7:15-16
Matthew 5:21-22	Romans 8:14
Matthew 5:27-30	Romans 10:9-10
Matthew 7:1-2	I Corinthians 4:1
Matthew 9:36	I Corinthians 5:12-13
Luke 5:32	I Corinthians 6:8
Luke 8:1-3	I Corinthians 6:9-11
Luke 8:13	I Corinthians 7:3
Luke 17:26	2 Corinthians 4:5

2 Corinthians 4:12

2 Corinthians 10:4

Galatians 3:26

Ephesians 1:19-21

Ephesians 5:3

Philippians 1:6

Philippians 4:8

Philippians 4:13

Titus 2:11-13

James 2:8-11

James 3:2

James 4:7

I Peter 5:8-9

2 Peter 2:20

1 John 4:4

Jude verse 7